Praise

What a joy it is to finally have Marquitta Lloyd's/Poetess P.R.Y.D.E poems in a collection I can carry with me and read whenever I want, to hear words that gift with humor, honesty, romance, and inspiration. Maquitta poems are fresh and clear, often fun, many times prayerful, and always accessible. Her rhyme schemes are original, amusing, tongue-in-cheek, and unpredictable.

After my book of poems, *Friends My Poems Gave Me*, was published by World Stage Press in 2016, Marquitta and I worked together in a writing group that focused specifically on our performance skills. She rose to the instruction and challenge, and won L.A.'s 2017 Women's Poetry Slam, to much acclaim. During this experience, I came to appreciate her sense of humor, thanks to her poem about dating, "Mind Over Madness," in which she says, "But there seems to be a drought when it comes to traditional ways," and the romantic nature of her poems, such as "He Da One," in which she admits, "He make my smile a bit crooked, and I almost appear bashful." Marquitta seeks honesty and newness in her life and expresses this search beautifully in her poem "The Visitors," when she writes, "Dear God," I cried out, "please make me new." And also, in my favorite poem, "Is It Saturday Yet?" as she states, "I prefer a true friendship over true fakeness."

Every time I hear Marquitta read or perform one of her poems at an event or open mic, I wind up smiling, snapping my fingers, and shaking my head in affirmation of her talents. Do not miss this opportunity to read her new book.

Charlie Becker

Poetess P.R.Y.D.E. has managed to create a balm made of words becoming the antidote for the pain that life's situations once left her heart and soul in. This beautifully written book of poetry will take you on a journey of highs and lows, with moments of strength and honesty. Between these pages are transparent and heartfelt truths, uncovering layers of mental and emotional trauma that have grown her into a willful and determined survivor.

Ms. LaLa DeVille

Poetess P.R.Y.D.E. literally undresses before us on these pages, disrobing fear and discarding garments that no longer fit the woman she is. She peels away old skin, revealing a woman who has evolved into a goddess. "Love Called in Sick Today" lets you know she ain't falling for the "rope-a-dope." "Girl Crush" reveals the difficult journey she has taken for self-acceptance and empowerment. Poems like "Daddy" are honest and reveal truth reserved for family. Through these pages, Poetess walks us through her awakening. Read these poems and join her journey.

Conney Williams

P.R.Y.D.E.

in
PRINT

**Penned by
Marquitta Lloyd**

P.R.Y.D.E.

in
PRINT

PRYDE IN P. R. I. N. T.
© 2019 Marquitta Lloyd
ISBN-13: 978-1-94-971314-5
First Edition, 2019
All rights reserved. No part of this publication may be reproduced, distributed, or transmitted in any form or by any means, including photocopying, recording, or other electronic or mechanical methods, without the prior written permission of the publisher, except in the case of brief quotations embodied in critical reviews and certain other noncommercial uses permitted by copyright law.
Printed in the United States of America

Layout Design by Nadia Hunter Bey
Cover Design by Anne Cercone

TABLE OF CONTENTS

POWERFUL and passionate pleasure for your mind, body, and soul

A Lifetime	9
Better Than Ice Cream	22
He Da One	23
I Am in Love	25
Man Undercover	26
Strings	28
You	30

RESILIENT because family, whether they are positive or negative, will help you bounce back

DADDY	34
MOMMY	36
My Ancestors Were Royalty	38
Oceans Run Deep in Heaven	39
The Hood	41

YOUNG and restless, vibrant at heart, with a seasoned soul

Acceptance	46
A Place Called Home	48
Eyes on Vermont	50
Fear Found Me	51
Girl Crush	52

Haters	53
I Know Why You Said Goodbye	55
I'm Dying to Live	58
I Quit	60
Is It Saturday Yet?	62
I Will Love You No More	63
Love Called in Sick Today	64
Mind Over Madness	66
Mistaken Identity	69
Money	70
My Addiction	72
Now Hiring!	74
Paralyze	76
Sense-less	77
The Truth	78
Wherever You Find It	79
Where My Secret Lies	80

DETERMINED not to let anger or frustration consume me

A Person in Pieces	84
Breaking News	88
Can't Poet For You	90
Destruction Meant for Instruction	92
Haiku	97
Heartbreak Hotel	98
He Couldn't Finish…	100
He Was…	101
I Heard You Were Leaving	102
Massacre	104

My Heart	106
My Life Lesson	107
Passing the Graveyard	110
Thank You for Changing My Life	112
That Chick	115
This Is Some Bullsh**!	118
When the Pain Is All Over You	120

ENCOURAGED by prayer, the church, and God

Conversations with the Devil	124
I Don't Fit In	126
Just Call on Jesus	129
Life Support	130
Love Lost	132
My Brother…My Sister	136
My Prayer	137
No One Is Bigger Than God	138
Now I Pray to Love	140
Our Gift	142
Peace	143
The Sermon	144
The Visitors	146

Introduction

I wrote my first poem when I was 15 years old. At the time, I was simply expressing a heartbreak, one that I thought was the worst thing in the world! After reviewing what I had written, I had to pat myself on the back because it rhymed and it sounded pretty intellectual. I had no idea the journey I was about to take, simply because I wrote my feelings down.

My first experience with poetry was when I heard Dr. Seuss's *The Cat in the Hat*, followed by *Hop on Pop* and *Green Eggs and Ham*. These rhythmic children's stories set the foundation for this L.A. native chocolate girl, who was raised by her grandmother, aunts, uncles, and mother. Life began to quickly turn into experiences that I had to immediately document. It wasn't until later that I realized I could possibly be a poet, especially after hearing my melodic phrases and comparing them to those of Langston Hughes and Maya Angelou. A friend read my work and decided to drag me to an open mic. I was never afraid to perform on stage; after all, I was never shy in front of an audience. But performing my deepest inner thoughts to perfect strangers was a new, natural high that overcame me. One open mic led to another and another, until this addiction led to a class that encouraged me to put my poems in a book. I created my stage name, Poetess P.R.Y.D.E., long before I thought of putting a book together. When I discovered the class, my book title, *P.R.Y.D.E. in Print*, was birthed.

One might find himself or herself within the pages of *P.R.Y.D.E. in Print*, just as one might believe himself or herself to be **Powerful, Resilient, Young, Determined,** and **Encouraged** — like I am. Enjoy!

P.R.Y.D.E.

in
PRINT

powerful
and passionate pleasure for your mind, body, and soul

A Lifetime

36 years, 4 months, 20 days, and 2 and a half hours

That's how long it took for him to find me
It seems like a lifetime

He met me at my worst
I learned him at his best
I was his company for the evening
And he was my guest, per our request

After he greeted me with a lengthy hug
He grabbed my hand and held it tight
I was nervous, and I was anxious, too
But this moment we shared felt just right

I was glad that I came
And he felt just the same
It took a long time for him to find me
It seems like a lifetime

Eventually, he placed his arms around my shoulder
And I found my arm around his back
If he was trying to impress me
Then he was most definitely on track

I needed him to know I was feeling him
I was hoping he got the hint
I think the feelings were mutual
And I'm assuming that's what he meant

I was glad that I came
And he felt just the same
It took a long time for him to find me
It seems like a lifetime

Protecting me on the sidewalk and opening my door

He was a gentleman, without a doubt
I'm pretty sure that if he didn't want to be there
He definitely would have changed his route

As we walked and we conversed
I could hear from us genuine laughter
And then a calm closeness came over us
And we bonded soon after

I was glad that I came
And he felt just the same
It took a long time for him to find me
It seems like a lifetime

I only wished time could slow down
I didn't want this date to end
Not only did I meet a handsome guy
But I made a brand-new friend

We had several conversations by phone
Before the day came to meet face to face
And when the day finally arrived
I found myself desiring to be in his space

I was glad that I came
And he felt just the same
It took a long time for him to find me
It seems like a lifetime

I was sneezing, stuffy, and just plain yucky sick
He was kind, considerate, and quick with me to click

From the moment we laid eyes on each other
We were immediately attached to one another

For the brief time that we shared
It seemed like he truly cared

In a moment, I seemed to have learned so much And it made me want to stay in touch

Had I known this man for a lifetime?
No, only for a very short time

His performance deserves an Oscar, an Emmy
And a Grammy
But here's the catch
He lived somewhere in Miami

36 years, 4 months, 20 days, and 2 and a half hours
That's how long it took for him to find me
It seems like a lifetime

Better Than Ice Cream

Can I tell you what's better than ice cream?
It's slippery and definitely wet
Hard and shaped funny.
It feels good between our lips, but it doesn't have much of a flavor. Right ladies?
That never stops us from sucking it!
I heard it feels good going down —
Down my spine, down my throat, your pleasure.
It's truly clear and it can be a bit sticky.
This is better than vanilla, chocolate, sherbet, or strawberry, even mint.
On the hottest hot summer day, it's the best time to suck...on...an ice cube.

He Da One

He be dat sweat rest'n' 'tween my thighs on a hot summer day
My heartbeat pounding like somebody knock'n' on the door
He got my hands trembling like a 5.0 earthquake in L.A.
And my mouth is dry like the desert full of cacti galore

Could he be da one?
He da one

He make my smile a bit crooked, and I almost appear bashful
I'm winking my eye once, twice, three times, and four
My lips blowing him a kiss, waiting for him to catch it
If he catch all my kisses, is he really keeping score?

Could he be da one?
He da one

He got me flirting a little when I raise one eyebrow at a time
Making sure he see me, but knowing I see him more
He got me singing sweet tunes to the sound of music
I'm singing loud, so loud, my throat is becoming sore

Could he be da one?
He da one

He be them floating butterflies in my stomach, flying so free
He got me suspended in midair, a feeling I can't ignore
Why, even my hair is beginning to react to his energy
It won't lay; it won't curl. So what else does he have in store?

Could he be da one?
He da one

He be dat arch in my back to release this sexual tension
And how come he don't know he got me nailed to the floor?
He got my nose open so wide, you could see into my brain
Now I know that ain't sexy, and that's nothing you'd want to explore
Could he be da one?

He da one

He make my breasts pay attention whenever he come near
Pressing heavy against my shirt, like tides press against the shore
He be dat buckle in my knees when I hear his voice in my ear
I'm hanging on to his every word, even if my hearing a bit poor

Could he be da one?
He da one

He got my neck and shoulders rotating. 'Cause what else will they do?
He be dat bend in my elbow, striking in and out, ready for a love war
He be dat stretch in my ankles even while I'm standing still
My toes might be dancing in my shoes for an encore
My hips swinging in his direction, hoping he'd dance with me
I'm feeling him like a lion feels his ultimate roar

Could he be da one?
He da one

He be dat perfect stranger that became a fond fellow
When all he did to me was say "Hello."

I Am in Love

You have the most gorgeous eyes, so warm and so full of love
Marble shaped and dark, round as the eye of a dove

When I look into those eyes of yours, I am sure that I am hypnotized
You don't even have to speak; it is then that I realize

I am in love

You have the sexiest lips; one kiss and I can't wait to do it again
I smile and then you smile; I finally kiss you once more, and then

You tell me you don't want to leave, and I pray to God you never do
I feel it's my responsibility to keep you satisfied the whole night through

I am in love

You have the strongest arms, and I feel so safe when you're holding me
Arms so heavy, muscular, and bold; I'd hate to be blind and never see

The joy you bring when you're around makes me forget all hurt and pain
You change my frown into a smile and give me sunshine instead of rain

I am in love

Man Undercover

You will never know his name
the first or the last
From where he came
could be the future or the past

He never wears the same thing twice
whether it be red or blue
This fellow is quite nice
his type is almost brand new

You see him in your dreams
he's your favorite lover
He comes by no other means
because he's the man undercover

You know him when you see him
because his smile lights up the place
It's brighter than any gem
you'll never forget his face

His walk is not at all strange
he just steps with pride
You hope his walk doesn't change
when you see him coming, step aside

You see him in your dreams
he's your favorite lover
He comes by no other means
because he's the man undercover

His voice can send chills
up and down your spine
He'll tell you how he feels
and leave you on cloud nine

Sometimes his hair is long

and sometimes it's not
His stylish hair is never wrong
though his hair isn't all he's got

You see him in your dreams
he's your favorite lover
He comes by no other means
because he's the man undercover

His body is structured in such a way
that it will make you want to cry
To touch his muscles will make your day
his curves will leave you floating high

He smells really good
his cologne is his body scent
And if you could
you'd give him a sexy hint

You see him in your dreams
he's your favorite lover
He comes by no other means
because he's the man undercover

Strings

How dare you say to me that now we can have sex
Assuming no emotions would be involved because now I'm your ex
So you wanna sleep with me and then move on to the next?
I suggest you go after the homegirl I saw in your text

While you're thinking with the head between your legs
I'm thinking with the head between my ears
And because my heart gets so involved
I find myself left drowning in my own tears

You don't want no strings to be attached
When you begin to remove my shirt
Then you unbutton my jeans so politely
When you didn't even think to flirt

You don't want no strings to be attached
When you're sucking my breasts, the left one and the right
But be careful not to use your teeth
Because I don't want you to accidentally bite

You don't want no strings to be attached
When you're licking on the side of my neck
Then I feel you blowing in my ear
Then you give my forehead a tender peck

You don't want no strings to be attached
When you're pulling me close to you
Gripping me and lifting me off the bed
And my body responds like this is brand new

You don't want no strings to be attached
When you run your fingertips alongside my waist
When you run your tongue across my navel
And then kiss me Frenchly, to give me a taste

You don't want no strings to be attached

When you're inside of me so deep
Going in and out, fast then slow
This will surely put my ass to sleep

You don't want no strings to be attached
When you flip me over as fast as you can
And then I back that thang up into you
Because after all, I am your biggest fan

You don't want no strings to be attached
When you're kissing the curve of my back
Now I'm bracing myself because if I know you
Then I know I need to get ready for a sexual attack

You don't want no strings to be attached
When we lie nude and play under the sheet
And when we're both done and we've both come
You'll lie across my sweaty chest to hear my heartbeat

This is the lovemaking we'll have only in your dreams
Because you won't be getting no more of this
I'm ending our affair with a nice hug
And I'm sealing it with a kiss

Unfortunately, we are no longer on the same page
I have to move on to bigger and better things
Because you just wanna have emotionless sex
But I have a heart...and I come with strings

You

I eat you

I drink you

I sleep, blink, and think you

I see you

I hear you

I smell you

I feel you

Then I kill you — with kindness

I hide you

Then I seek you

I find you

Then I keep you

I make you

I mold you

I kiss you

Then I hold you

I fight with you

Then I'm friends with you

It starts with you

And it ends with you

I dream of you

I love you

I place no one above you

I inhale you and exhale you
I sure do breathe you

Then I turn around and I bleed you

resilient

because family, whether they are positive or negative, will help you bounce back

DADDY

I look around me, and I envy some of my friends and relatives so
Because they have something that I've never had to show
Actually, it's a person that's been part of their lives for a while
This person was there when they cried, and this person was there to help them smile

Daddy, where were you when I needed you most?
About you I can never brag, and about you I can never boast

Daddy, where were you when I brought my first certificate home?
I wanted you to see it. I looked for you. Where did you roam?

Daddy, where were you when I earned a trophy of gold
For winning the spelling bee? I got it in 1989, so now it's old

Daddy, where were you when I brought home my first "A,"
Then "B," and then "C"? I couldn't show you anyway

Daddy, where were you when I went to the seventh grade —
Junior high, in other words? I got through it without you as I prayed

Daddy, where were you when I had questions about boys?
I wanted to know, were they smart, did they have poise?

Daddy, where were you when I needed you to help me
With my homework, for example? That's okay; I got help from my auntie

Daddy, where were you when I joined a martial-arts class?
The whole thing was based on self-defense, a test I eventually passed

Daddy, where were you when I became a cheerleader?
Did I mention I loved to dance? This girl, you have to meet her

Daddy, where were you when I went to my prom?
You should have seen me; I looked bomb!

Daddy, where were you when I graduated from high school?
Everyone was there to congratulate me; if you weren't there, you're a fool

Daddy, where were you when I needed a father-daughter talk?

Daddy, where were you when I wanted to go with you for a walk?

Daddy, where were you when I was trying college for the first time?
I was so terrified, but my grandma stood by me; now everything's fine

Daddy, where were you when I needed some money?
I thought I could depend on you, raining or sunny

Daddy, where were you when I got my first job?
You weren't there to cheer me on, and so I had to sob

Daddy, will you be there when I go into my career?
I want to be a school teacher, so have no fear

Daddy, will you be there to give me away
To walk me down the aisle on my wedding day?

Daddy will you be there when I give birth to my first baby?
I always dreamed that you would, maybe, just maybe

Daddy, will you be there…will you be in my life at all,
So that I can be proud, so that I can stand tall?

Daddy, will you be there…?

MOMMY

Like the Lord is my shepherd
You are my mother
I shall not have another

Like the Lord leads me beside the still waters
You guide me
And you hide me

Like the Lord restores my soul
You relate to the way I think
And you're always the missing link

The Lord made a great sacrifice
And for our lives He paid the price
I was a gift to you, and you to me
No one else would have ever been so nice

He has shown us His love
Just as He blesses a simple dove
He allowed an angel to rest on you
Truly an angel from above

You are my best friend
And I can't even pretend
I know you loved me from the beginning
And I know you'll love me until the end

Just like the Lord, you loved me from the start
So I always recognized your heart
And if I had it my way
We'd never ever be apart

Mommy, you mean the universe to me
I want nothing more than for you to see
God has brought us a mighty long way

If it weren't for the Lord, where would we be?

So I celebrate you today
In the most beautiful way
Lord, I thank You for my mommy
And that's all I have to say

My Ancestors Were Royalty

Someone told me my ancestors were royalty
Maybe they were
I'll never know

But can we start with the nearest ancestor
whom you might call my father?
I call him a sperm donor
who loaned my mother a squirt or two
But, surprise!
I won the race
You can't put me back!
Where the hell are you?
Who are you?
What are you doing with your life that gives you the right to leave me out of it?

Someone told me my ancestors were royalty
Maybe they were
I'll never know

As for me, I will be the royal one in this generation of my family
They will love me
Bless me
Hug me
Kiss me
But you do not deserve the name of my "ancestor"
"Ancestors" are generally descendants from past times
You will be discussed in past tense
Because you chose not to be present
So your absence made me who I am

Thanks

Oceans Run Deep in Heaven

I heard oceans run deep in the South, but ain't nobody swimming there
Instead, somebody drowning
Them bodies of water too deep, and anybody in their right mind
just gone watch that ocean from a distance
I don't live in the South, but I do live in South Central
And there ain't no swimming for me in South Central
If I go to the local park, I might grab my bathing suit and stand in 5 feet deep
cuz I'm almost scared to go under
If I go to my uncle's place, I'll get in his pool and push off the wall with my bare feet
That's where I practice swimming
cuz ain't nobody ever taught me how to do it
Ain't no swimming in my bathtub; I'm too big and my tub is too small
After I'm done with thinking about the water, standing in the water
Playing in the water, and trying to swim in the water,
I think about how it must've been in my mother's womb
Did I swim there?
Well, I can't go back to find out. But the next phase of this life will still have water in it
When I leave this earth, I'm gonna be the best swimmer there ever was
Cuz I was never no good swimmer here on Earth
Cuz nobody, not Mama, not Daddy, not Grandma or Grandpa, not Uncle, Auntie
or Cousin ever tried to teach me. Once, one of my students tried teaching me
while we were in the city pool. He pulled me and I kicked; he pulled; I kicked
He pulled some more, and I kicked harder until I found myself in sudden panic mode

My leg caught a spasm and I suddenly went under. I thought my life was ending

until the lifeguard and a co-worker pulled me up from the water and I reached for a deep breath

In tears, I was carried to the side of the pool. My co-worker then massaged

that stubborn cramp out of my leg. I just remember crying and my heart beating fast

That year, I vowed to never get in the pool again, let alone anybody's ocean

But years later, I tried again, to swim, that is

When I leave this earth, I'm gonna swim and swim and swim, cuz oceans run deep in heaven

The Hood

The doctor pulled me out and said, "It's a girl."
And my babyhood began

My hair was short, dark, and curly
So Mama twisted it and added pink barrettes and red bows
She'd take the suction and clean my nose
Put powder in my diaper to make me smell like a fresh rose
Played with my fingers and kissed all my toes
Then took pictures of me whenever I had the cutest pose
And that's how my story goes...
That was my babyhood
I wish I could — I sho' 'nuff would — go back to babyhood
Back then, it was all good

I think I was five when I had my first birthday party
And my girlhood began

That's when I got dresses of all colors
Pink ones with flowers: red, yellow, orange, and lavender; it's true
I don't remember if I got anything blue
Maybe a pair of cute jeans came new
And the socks with the ruffles, I got more than two
I was in heaven. What else was a girl to do?
I had a wonderful view....
That was my girlhood
I wish I could — I sho' 'nuff would — go back to girlhood
Back then, it was all good

By now, I had been going to school for a few years
And my childhood began

I started to bring home homework and report cards
I had participated in my first science fair
I started combing my own hair
And I could pick out what I wanted to wear
Now I had feelings of what I looked like; I began to care

Because boys started to look at me and stare
And something was in the air...
That was my childhood
I wish I could — I sho' 'nuff would — go back to childhood
Back then, it was all good

My body was going through some changes
And my teenhood began

Just in time for this video about "girls"
I am a girl and I'm not ashamed
But this video is making me feel like I'm to blame
The people in this video don't even know my name
But they're telling me from where my breasts came
And they got the nerve to give this bloodshed some fame
Now all the girls are feeling the same: embarrassed....
That was my teenhood
I wish I could — I sho' 'nuff would — go back to teenhood
Back then, it was all good

Now I recognized all the changes, good and bad
And my womanhood began

Now I'm getting into this thing called life
Learning that problems come again and again
Distinguishing the boys from the men
Questioning the God above: who, what, why, how, and when?
Raised in the church but didn't know back then
That the older I would get, the more I might sin
Breathing and counting to ten...
That was my womanhood
I wish I could — I sho' 'nuff would — go back to womanhood
Back then, it was all good

Finally I was older and I was wiser
And my ladyhood began

I can now say I've been through some things

I remember when I couldn't wait to be grown
But those days are long gone
Mama said stay a child as long as you can, and watch your tone
Throwing tantrums and wanting to be left alone
Then I'd call my so-called boyfriend on the phone
I'm telling him I wanna run away; he telling me he wants to bone

Reminiscing during my ladyhood
I can honestly say now that I understood
Mama warned me as best she could
And taught this girl like a woman should
Not how to be a princess
But how to display my queenhood...

And now, it's all good

young

and restless, vibrant at heart, with a seasoned soul

Acceptance

I accept things that come and go fast
So things that come slowly will last and last

I accept that even those closest to me won't always be my best friend
So I am my own best friend, and I'll be my own best friend until the end

I accept haters that come my way too
So people who sincerely love me will stay true

I accept always falling in love when love never falls in me
So what's hidden in plain sight will be easy for me to see

I accept my bills that follow me every time I pack up and move
So I give my check back to the collector, with nothing left to prove

I accept that I will take my debt to my grave
So I gave up on the idea of how much money I could save

I accept that sometimes I'm on the outside looking in
So when I feel like I've lost, I really did win

I accept tears that are silent behind my smile
So it doesn't affect my walk, my talk, or my exotic style

I accept that I don't have a Coca-Cola-bottle waistline
So I'll remember that my beautiful imperfections are still mine

I accept your honesty when you're ready to let me go
So you are brave enough to at least let me know

I accept that I have hypothyroidism and sometimes high cholesterol
So I can be reminded of good health, body and all

I accept that sometimes my poetry don't fit the crowd
So the crowd fits my poetry and I feel quite proud

I accept learning how to cope with disappointment
So I can conquer my own mistakes and live in enjoyment

I accept my undeniably exquisite, sexy, brown-skinned complexion
So I use my skin tone to give you a mental erection

I accept that sometimes this life deals me a bad hand
So I learn not to have fear when everything around me is sinking sand

I accept all things that make me insecure
So even with my insecurities, of myself I can still be sure

I accept all of my flaws, the ones I hate and the ones you hate more
So I can check myself, be myself, and still love myself to the core

I accept that all my daddy ever did was loan my mama some of his sperm
So she knows, I know, and everybody in this room knows he was just short term

I accept that the more I live, the closer I get to death
So I laugh hard and I talk loud with every given breath

I, Poetess P.R.Y.D.E., do solemnly swear to accept me, the whole me, and nothing but me

A Place Called Home

Public-school teachers are always on strike because the pay doesn't match their work ethic.

Three different ice cream trucks drive down my street on a Saturday.

I'm riding in the car with Mama, wondering why the woman on the street with the fishnet leggings is waving at the honking cars.

The man on the news channel tells me that a corner store was robbed today, and two were injured.

How would your family survive this place?

I still wonder how I survived this place,
this place I call...home.

I've never lived outside of the state, but I've lived in a couple of different cities,

Always wondering what it would be like to live in Atlanta, Georgia.

What would it be like to live in New Orleans, Louisiana?

Or even Baton Rouge?

What would it be like to live in Dallas, Texas?

What would it be like to live in Las Vegas, Nevada?

After all, these are places I've visited throughout my life.

But in the famous words of Dorothy: "There's no place like home."

How would your family survive this place?

I still wonder how I survived this place,
this place I call...home.

Yeah, it can be quite a dangerous place to live at times.

I remember my sister and I having a discussion with a couple, who asked,

"How can you live in a place where there are earthquakes? Aren't you afraid of falling underground?"

While my sister and I asked,

"How can you live in a place where there are tornadoes? Aren't you afraid of getting thrown into another town?"

If you weren't born and raised here, I guess you'll never know.

And I wouldn't be able to explain it to you, to make you understand.

Some live with tornadoes; some live with tsunamis and floods.

Some live with hurricanes.

However, I live with dealers, murderers, rapists, thieves, drunk drivers, kidnappers, and earthquakes.

But L.A. is home to me.

Eyes on Vermont

The last time I walked into this business
I was getting my eyes checked for contact lenses

Six years have now passed
Now I'm rushing into the building fast

I'm past due for my eyes to be checked
And a new pair of glasses it's time to select

So I'm entering the building once again
Six years later, will I run into an old friend?

I complete my paperwork and take it to the front
While I'm wondering what kind of frame I want

About 50 minutes later, the eye doctor calls my name
As I enter the room, I realize it looks the same

I sit in the chair and remove my eyewear
The doctor then clears my eyes with a puff of air

I'm sure you know exactly what happened next
Letters on the wall, she asks, "Can you read the text?"

I squint and I moan because I can't see
The eye doctor asks again, "Can you read the letters to me?"

When I begin to mumble the squiggly figures
"F, A, D, R, B," I'm disturbed by my triggers

"Just tell me what I need to know and return my glasses, please."
After telling me I'm nearsighted, she picks up my glasses with ease

Unfortunately, she didn't tell me anything new
"Now get me some clear glasses to see through."

Fear Found Me

It always
Worried me
And made me afraid
To try new things. Anxiety is
An understatement. It kept me from
Being talked into anything I am not used to
Or anything I have never done before. It made me
Sweat from misconception, and made my hands shake
uncontrollably. Let's not forget to mention my heart that would beat
twice as fast as it normally beats. Fear found me. Now the butterflies
have left my stomach, slowly crawled down both my thick thighs,
skipped across both my bended knees, danced a cute little cha-cha in my
legs, traveling to the back of both my heavy calves. My shins embraced
the butterflies as they fancy-flipped a great cartwheel into my left
foot, then into my right, and I admit, it tickled just a bit. I
thought they were gone, but they finally landed in my
ten toes, one by one by one. Now I am unable to
breathe because the idea of it all has
completely
taken
my
breath
away.

Girl Crush

If I ever gave in to this feeling
she'd know that she was more than enough for me
She was tough, like the thick rubber on a tire
Yeah, she was that tough and could take anything
Pretty tough but pretty gentle to the soul
Like the beauty of a rainbow after a storm has washed the city clean
I love her; I do.

But if I ever gave in to this feeling
she'd know just how much she really meant to me
Day after day, thoughts of her are a reflection of my well-being
my smile, my walk and my talk, my hands, how I wear my hair, my eyes, even my feet
If I ever gave in to this feeling
she'd be full of fire, the fire that's ignited within, and she'd burn with passion of desire
not sexually, but lovingly because she would know without a doubt that she…
is…
me

Haters

Lawyers defend their clients
The guilty don't want to take the blame
Doctors take care of the sick
And the haters earn their name

Electricians work with wires
Thieves are meant to rob
Pastors preach from the Bible
And the haters are on their job

Mechanics can fix your car
Stylists perform magic on your hair
Teachers educate the children
And the haters just don't care

Construction workers build things
Verizon services your cell phone
Bus drivers carry the passengers
And the haters won't leave you alone

The artists create paintings
The chefs can fry and bake
Photographers take great pictures
And the haters are still fake

Actors can put on a show
Runners are made to run track
Librarians care for their books
And the haters just attack

The florists care for the plants and flowers
Investigators solve the crime
The police officers make arrests
And the haters are always on time

The trainers help get you in shape
The psychiatrists help you regain your pride
The speakers help motivate the listener
And the haters like to hide

The farmers plant in the fields
The fire fighters put out the fire
The disc jockeys play the latest hits

And the haters don't retire

The musicians play their instruments
The judge makes the rule
The singers hit a high note
And the haters are still cruel

I didn't mention every profession
But I mentioned quite a few
I have a job; you have a job
And the haters have a job, too!

So if you think you're a hater
Ask for forgiveness on your knees
A hater can be frowned on
So don't be a hater, please

But if you must be a hater, hate on me
I know your job is to prey on me and tease
Otherwise, how else will He prepare
A table in the presence of my enemies?

I Know Why You Said Goodbye

I know why you had to go
I know why you said goodbye
You didn't want me to hurt
You didn't want me to cry

Your destiny is never tied
To anybody that left, I read
True statements by TD Jakes
You'll go left; I'll go right instead

God knows what's best for me
He's got something better in mind
For me He's got something special
Because He's just that kind

Won't ask for anyone more fair
Placing my feelings ahead of yours
But it still hurts so bad
When it rains, it pours

You were good to me
Protecting me, I can tell
Everything that glitters ain't gold
But you were shiny as hell

You told me I deserved better
I misunderstood what you meant
You put the signs in my face
I refused to take the hint

Feeling bad about your decision
It was best for both of us
So if that's the case, my friend
I'll stop making a fuss

Your loss and my loss too
Unequal on every level

You lose, another gains
Victory's not for the devil

I heard if I set you free
And you return a second time
Then you'll know that I'm yours
And I'll know that you are mine

But I'm certain that this is it
No getting back together again
We broke up and made up twice
Let's bring this affair to an end

Your chapter in my life is over
Everything happens for a reason
After all, nothing lasts forever
I'm told pain lasts for a season

I'll quote TD Jakes once more
He so eloquently said, "LET IT GO!"
If someone better is waiting
I should be the first to know

I'll turn this negative positive
In time my heart will heal
My hurting will be a memory
This is God's will

Loneliness is unbearable
The pain is extremely intense
Keep busy and stay focused
That's what makes sense

Thank you for saying goodbye
You did what you felt was best
I cannot call you selfish
God put you to the test

Will you do the right thing?

Even if we didn't understand
We are to depend on Him
Our problems should go in His hand

Putting all attention on me
Take my focus off you
Return to who I am
Concentrate on all I do
Looking ahead, it's true
My windshield is much bigger
Than my rearview

I'm Dying to Live

I'm dying to live...
I'm dying to live...

I'm dying to live...don't you see?
I'm dying to be seen like the people on T.V.
Getting paid to memorize my lines, whether I have 30 or 3
I want to be someone else when I can't be me

I'm dying to live...don't you know?
I'm dying to flow like so-and-so on the radio
I can sing a song fast or I can sing a song slow
My notes can be high or my notes can be low

I'm dying to live...without fear
I'm dying to dance to the music I hear
Tunes in my head from far and near
Can you dance with me, my dear?

I'm dying to live...by grace
I'm dying to own my own place
In my own home I'll be in the mortgage race
And it's the world I'll be able to face

I'm dying to live...mild
I'm dying to have a family with a husband and child
This should keep me from behaving wild
In hopes that a divorce never gets filed

I'm dying to live...on a bet
I'm dying to be bill free and get out of debt
I want to escape the financial net
And I refuse to accept a harmful threat

I'm dying to live...light
So I hit the gym so my body can be tight
Doctors say that I'm overweight for my height
So I try my best, but it's hard to eat right

I'm dying to live
I'm dying to be loved
He might be dying to be loved
She might be dying to be loved
  I AM DYING TO BE LOVED

Or maybe...I'm...just...dying!

I Quit

The good thing about this company is that they're always hiring
Truly, honestly, rarely ever firing

Substitutes are needed in preschool when a teacher is absent
So the substitute does what is absolutely meant

No general supervisor, only a representative I reported to
And I dare not reveal the company name to you

If I'm not very successful, maybe I'll be back
I'm moving forward to something that'll put me on track

To whom this may concern:

A, B, C, D, E, F, G,
H, I, J, K, L, M, N, O, P,

Q, R, S, T, U, V,
W, X, Y and Z

Now I know my ABCs
No more kids will pee on me!

I would get in trouble if a kid sat on my knee
The kids don't listen. Can't you see?

Yellow and blue make green
And I could never make enough of that mean green
Yet, my master's degree went unseen
Because they're preschoolers; I'd never work with a teen

The preschoolers are learning patterns while counting, coloring, and finally...sleeping
You definitely will never catch me weeping
But my composure I'm constantly keeping
Lucky for you, I haven't run away from here, leaping
The kids wake up and begin to cry

And that's when I begin to sigh
I'm not gonna lie
Today I'm saying goodbye

I will no longer worry if they don't share
I'm not saying that I don't care
But come on now, let's be fair
These kids will fight and they will swear

Friends will still play on the playground
This is true, and you know what else I've found?
They'll kick the ball and you'll hear a sound
As for me, I will be nowhere around

After lunch, they may read books or play with toys
The girls will play with the girls, and the boys with the boys
Preschoolers will forever make much noise
To the teacher, it brings gentle joys

But today, I quit; hooray, I'm free!
Now you know what is to be
As I sit back and sip my tea
Don't be a hater; congratulate me
I Quit

Is It Saturday Yet?

Is it Saturday yet?
Mad Mondays got my mind mesmerized, and I might be making excuses, but don't misunderstand me. I wanna make my money; I just don't wanna go to work. Them dollars might be motivational if my job were more recreational. But I maneuver hour by hour, and it's a miracle that I make it out alive!

Is it Saturday yet?
Terrible Tuesdays got me trippin' because this twenty-something-year-old keep testing me and trying my patience. I'm too mature for this. The teenagers keep talkin' back, and I'm so tired of that. Instead of being treated, I'm being tricked, and I thought tricks were for kids.

Is it Saturday yet?
Weird Wednesdays got me writing wack words just to make it through the week. After all, it is hump day and I got two more days to go before my week ends, and I'm at my wits' end. I can't wait any longer. I wish I could work from home.

Is it Saturday yet?
Threatening Thursdays got me thinking that this job pays the bills, so I'd better be thankful. It's them against me, but in theory I'm thrilled to know tomorrow is Friday. Will I need therapy when it's all said and done?

Is it Saturday yet?
Foolish Fridays got me fighting for my faith that I'll return to this workplace next week. Sure, I have my freedom of speech, yet I fail to follow through with my fellow colleagues in saying, "Have a good weekend," because I really don't care if they do or not. I prefer a true friendship over true fakeness. Funny fact is even my calendar reads W T F.
Is it Saturday yet?

I Will Love You No More

When the rainbow falls out of the sky
When birds forget how to fly
When babies can no longer cry
I will love you no more

When the sun stops shining bright
When the stars fall out of sight
When there is darkness but no light
Continue to love you, what for?

When we no longer feel pain
When the earth receives no rain
When there's everything to lose and nothing to gain
I will love you no more

When there are no more shadows by our side
When there are no more coasters to ride
When there's no one left to guide
Continue to love you, what for?

When there is no more money to spend
When there is no help to lend
When there is no one to call a friend
I will love you no more

When there's no winter, spring, summer, or fall
When no tears can be shed at all
When bugs can no longer crawl
Continue to love you, what for?

Love Called in Sick Today

There weren't any butterflies to capture
I didn't float on cloud 9, 10, or 11
My hands didn't tremble at the sound of his voice
My voice didn't tremble at the sight of his face, because his face wasn't...well, it just wasn't
I didn't sweat...anywhere
I wouldn't let him hold my calm hands
His lips landed on my left cheek as I avoided lip to lip contact, and I felt...nothing
My heartbeat was...normal, nothing to be concerned about
I didn't want him to invite me out to dinner
The movies were out of the question, too dark and too intimate
He'd never see the inside of my place
I gave him patty-cake pats on the back as he went in for a hug, and my pelvic area kept a fair distance from his
My hair was freshly washed, but I wouldn't let him play in it or stroke it
I wore my favorite perfume
I forced space so he couldn't get close enough to smell my scent
I didn't let him wrap his hand around my waist
I avoided eye contact so he couldn't look me in my eyes when he talked to me
I didn't laugh at any of his jokes, and I didn't smile that often
I was dressed cute—hair and makeup on point, but I reluctantly accepted his compliments
I didn't get a glass slipper today
I didn't kiss a frog in hopes of finding a prince
My knees never buckled, and my toes never curled in my shoes
When the date was over, I returned to my place...alone, but not lonely
Checking my mailbox, I discovered a letter from Love
I hesitated when opening it, in fear that I would read my worst nightmare

It read:

This is Love,

I'm writing to inform you that you will go on a date that won't be to your liking. It won't meet your satisfaction, and you might be disappointed. But you'll be okay. I wanted to give you a heads-up. You won't be falling in Me today. I'm not feeling too well. Love is calling in sick today.

Truly not yours,

Not yet.

Signed, Love

Mind Over Madness

Have we begun to overrate
What we used to call a date?

What ever happened to men asking to take a woman out
And then actually taking her out?

I don't mean to pout
But there seems to be a drought
When it comes to traditional ways

Call me old fashioned, if you'd like, but I remember back in the days
A guy would pick a girl up and take her on a date

I see more men take women to court
Than I see women get courted
And I'm trying to get this sorted
In my head
Take me on a date before you try to take me to bed

Unfortunately, my shoulder does carry a chip
But if he's got the right salsa, we can go for a dip

I wanna hang out with a gentleman, not a gentle boy
And a good hang-out puts you in the mix
Nowadays, a date is considered going to his crib
And watching Netflix

Yeah, I called it a drought because there is a shortage of chivalry
But there's plenty of difficulty
And friendship is no longer on the agenda

If your money is funny and my change is strange
Let's do something cheap or almost free
A walk on the beach or a picnic at the park is absolutely fine with me

Window shopping at the mall, hiking, karaoke, or open-mic-night poetry
Yet I'm learning to enjoy my own company

Me, myself, and I, that's all I got in the end
Because these days a man doesn't want to be your friend

I got way too many exes and not enough whys to go around
I should have asked the right questions before we got down
And the second round only included, "What's up, Ma?" and a fist pound

Oh, but if he's really feelin' me, he'll ask if he can have a hug
And giving my shoulders a shrug
I sweep my concerns under the rug

Because all I want to do is go out
Now, is a good conversation in the passenger's seat of your car the best you can do?
Well, hell, I'll take it for now

Oh, I see, because I took it for now
That's a dead giveaway that I'll take it later, too?

Silly me, for thinking standards are sentences you rewrite repeatedly
And maybe even rapidly
For punishment's sake

When all along I was playing myself; I turned out to be the one that was fake
You kept it real with me all along

You went as far as I let you go
I should have been boss, set some high standards from jump
That way you couldn't say you didn't know

Well, I heard someone say better late than never
I want to go on a real date and enjoy a sweet endeavor
We can come up with an idea that's clever, together

Mind over madness, for the pursuit of happiness
Mind over madness, should I pursue happiness?
Mind over madness, I'm pursuing happiness
I'll take myself on a date; I'll take myself to dinner

I'll treat myself to a movie. I hear you saying, "Knock it off,"
Because you think I'm being artificial, like a real knock-off

But I'm being honest...with myself
I get lonely and I get sad
When I see other couples, I almost get mad

So can we please go on a date in real life?
Can I truly date myself?
No. Just like I can't be my own wife

                                         Honestly....

Mind over madness, for the pursuit of happiness
Mind over madness, should I pursue happiness?
Mind over madness, I'm pursuing happiness

Mistaken Identity

I'm thirty-something
My skin is brown colored
I'm a female, you see
Yet I have a mistaken identity

Am I the wrong age, wrong skin color?
Am I the wrong sex, thinking I was an impressionable beauty?
But I have a mistaken identity

Bet I know my times tables, at least up to eleven
I know how to read and I sho 'nuff know how to write
So I consider myself as smart as can be
I have a mistaken identity

I stand about 5'5" and I wear an 8.5 size shoe
My hair can be kinky, curly, or straight, and I wear glasses because I'm nearsighted
None of these ever stopped me
But I have a mistaken identity

My favorite color is turquoise, and I also love brown
My favorite hobbies include singing and dancing
All these things make me feel free
I have a mistaken identity

I have a name that's not easy to pronounce
I have a history that's not easy to admit
Was I supposed to be born a he rather than a she?
But I have a mistaken identity

Everything about me that you see is wrong
When it really doesn't make a difference what your opinion be. . .
I'm me, just me, truly
And your opinion is not my mistaken identity

Money

You come and you go, you
Come and you go, you...
You go to the gas station, the market, the car wash, the mechanic, and occasionally the DMV
But can we go to the movies, the next concert, the next stage play, or any live show, for that matter?
Let's go out to eat, skating, bowling, dancing, an amusement park, a trip — either by plane, bus, or train
I can't help it; I can't get enough of you, and when I seem to have too much of you
I got to hurry up and spend you
In addition to my 9 to 5, I'm part-time Lyft driving and all the time recycling — recycling cans, recycling plastic bottles, recycling my work hours just to complete and repeat the cycle of recycling and making money to live and eat. Or am I eating to live?
Before you get to my account, you get counted, deposited, and transferred
But it's preferred that I keep you
I pay my tithes and offerings with you
And you pay my bills for me too
Very rarely do you get spent on me...just me
I don't know...a new pair of shoes would be nice; a cute outfit might suffice
My hair and nails get neglected, so for those, I'm willing to pay the price
I know you're familiar with the dollar
Not the quarters that go to the laundromat, but the paper that goes to one of two places — the strip club or the church house — and I'll admit my dollar and I have been to both
That very dollar gets used and reused, I swear, because I see it everywhere, all the time, and it doesn't excite me
But if I accidentally find about three of them in my back pocket, woohoo, jackpot!
I just want you all to myself
Don't get me wrong; pennies, nickels, dimes, and quarters add up
But has anyone seen the 50-cent piece recently?
I was probably 12 years of age the last time that was placed in my hand
But ones, fives, tens, twenties, fifties, and hundred-dollar bills
All of these I've seen, but they go quicker than they come. Know what I mean?
I joke about these dead presidents, the moolah, the coins, paper, cash, currency, loot, dough
But the reality is there's a rumor going around that black people don't save money

That we barely get car insurance, let alone life insurance
Fathers are burying daughters
Mothers are burying sons
When it's time to bury our bodies, our babies, our loved ones
Are we really putting our dollars away for that rainy day?

My Addiction

To have any addiction, I know is wrong
But it's too late; I've already been addicted way too long
It's an addiction that I love to love
But don't you worry; this is not another love song

I want to tell you about my addiction today
But how long I've been addicted is too hard to say
I'm smart enough to know any addiction is not good
But I decided to go along with it anyway

Like any addiction, the risks are high
Concerning the side effects, I cannot tell a lie
Bad things can happen when you are an addict
Things so bad they cause your loved ones to cry

You may ask why I'm excited about this phase
And why I won't shake its wicked ways
I guess it's a different, yet mysterious, addiction
And it's not like I'm trapped in a difficult maze

No, really, I'm able to figure it out
It's easy to understand, no doubt
If you were in my shoes right now
Then you'd know exactly what I'm talking about

You're eager to hear about my addiction; I can tell
You want to know what happened and how I fell
Understand that this is not easy to explain
But you can't buy my story; it's not for sale

First, let me tell you what it does to my eyes
Whenever I see it, it causes my temperature to rise
Maybe you say that I should look away
But I know that wouldn't be wise

Next, I'll tell you what it does to my ears
It's actually quite harmless because it erases my fears

It allows me to listen to beautiful things
Voices and expressions that bring me happy tears

Now I'll tell you what it does to my tongue
It's become just as necessary as my right and left lung
I use it simultaneously with my mouth
And I feel all innocent, like I did when I was young

So I'll tell you now what it does to my mind
It causes me to think things awfully kind
Every time I use it, it's a different experience
And it makes me want to press rewind

Let's not forget what it does to my feet
It makes me take off into the street
Sometimes there's no real destination
But to me that's really pretty neat

Finally, I'll tell you the effect it has on my heart
My goodness, I don't know where to start
It skips a beat when I'm doing my thing
And I almost go crazy when my addiction and I are apart

I can't get around this addiction
I can't go under or above
What I can tell you about this addiction
Is that I'm addicted to your love

Now Hiring!

Are you trying to be my new boo?
Or are you trying to be my next ex?
Either way, if you think I'm gorgeous, if you think I'm beautiful, if you think I'm fine,
Then sign your name here on the dotted line

Are you applying for a position, to be employed by me?
You want me to supervise you and only you, exclusively?
You must think I'm gorgeous. Do you think I'm beautiful?
Maybe you think I'm fine. I don't know what you have in mind...but....

Take this application; fill it out completely
And when you're done with it, return it to me
No, you don't have to pay for this application; it's free
It's me you pay for; I ain't free, but I hold the key...
To your heart, that is, only if you qualify to be my next guy
I'm sorry — did you need help filling this form out?
Don't worry; when you're done, I'll know what you're all about

Let's start with your name, the first and the last
Unfortunately, this alone won't tell me about your past
Write your age here; I need to know how old you are
If you're too young for me, you won't get very far
Don't forget to add when you were born
Your birth month, day, and certainly the year
You never know what your sign may reveal to me, my dear
I can't let you forget to add your nationality and race
I need to know exactly who is in my face
Make sure you enter today's date; I must remember when you applied
And everything from here on out will show me if you've got something to hide
Include your C.D.L., or your California Driver's License, please
This might tell me if you're simply just a tease
Oh yes, has your license ever been revoked or suspended?
Do you attempt to renew what has ended?
What about your numerical Social Security?
Will it somehow reveal your personality?
What is the best time to reach you?
Add your number, including your area code
If I choose to dial, please don't put me on hold
Now I need you to add your likes, hobbies, and interests
If your interests include not enough work and too much rest,
Then you've already failed the test

Here, you need to tell me if you've ever been convicted of a felony or crime
A misdemeanor is just as bad, so I need to know if you've done some time
Now I need the background on your education
Did you graduate from high school? Did you go to college? I must know the situation
Do you have any type of certifications that you can add?
If you're licensed in something, I'll know if it's good or bad
Okay, think back to your last employment
Why do you find interest here? What do you think is different?
What were your duties at the last job you held?
What was your title? Tell me about a time when you failed
Add your references on this line below
So I can call all of the people you claim to know
Exactly what position are you applying for?
Because I'm not hiring a man-whore
How did you hear 'bout this job, by the way?
Because I don't advertise for this position every day
Have you applied for this position within the twelve months that has passed?
This will determine if you move too fast
Do you know someone who worked for me previously?
What did you find out about me? I take this job seriously
Last but not least, why are you applying to work for me?
Are you trying to see what you can get for free?
If you don't qualify, there will be no us, no we
Answer these questions to the best of your knowledge and maybe...
I will be your she and you will be my he
Will I actually be the lock to your key?
We'll just have to wait and see...what will be shall be
Don't call me; I'll call you if you get approved for an interview
Now that you've applied
I'll contact you if your application doesn't get denied

Paralyze

Overwhelming thoughts of you and me
paralyze
my
mind.

You and I aren't a pair of lies
but a pair of truths untold
I unfold
to let you in mentally, physically, spiritually, but seriously
I'm so into you, like SWV once said, and I once read
It's better to have loved and lost than to never have loved

I want to love with innocence rather than lose with no sense...of direction
That's nonsense, you would say, but in my defense
I'd much rather love you than hate you
No disguise can hide the outpour of cries used to express hellos and
goodbyes
Is there such a thing as goodbyes?

Why, of course!
Because without them, one denies how he or she survives the loss of girls
or the loss of guys in a relationship.
I'm wise enough
To size up the tough
Realities, the sighs
I exhale; even my lows are greater than my highs

My mind is in overload
I die with every try
Becoming more
and more
and more
paralyzed
knowing we aren't a pair of lies
but a pair of truths untold

Sense-less

She called me sound, not because I could speak, not because my voice was loud and obnoxious, but because I had a voice that was quiet and patient, like the subtle wind that blows so calmly. And I could hear everything and nothing all at the same time as I fight to survive.

She called me sight, not because my eyes were big and brown, but because I had a vision to see the beauty of the world, like the blue skies and the distant mountains. And I could see everything and nothing all at the same time as I fight to survive.

She called me taste, not because my tongue has taste buds, but because I had a nature that was as sweet as the peach cobbler Grandma used to make for me. And I could taste everything and nothing all at the same time as I fight to survive.

She called me touch, not because my two hands could feel yours, but because I had feelings that could reach your soul, like the emotions of happiness, sadness, and everything in between. And I could touch everything and nothing all at the same time as I fight to survive.

She called me smell, not because my nose could sniff and blow, but because I had nostrils that breathed in the aroma around me, that smelled to me like a field of flowers. And I could smell everything and nothing all at the same time as I fight to survive.

None of this makes sense, but these senses are consistent. There's persistence in my existence as I fight to survive in a world that's senseless and that's no nonsense.

The Truth

I see the white of your eyes
So tell me no lies
I see the white of your eyes
And you see the tears in mine
So tell me the truth
Do you know me?

I see the white of your eyes
And it's no surprise
I see the white of your eyes
And you see the fear in mine
So tell me the truth
Do you see me?

I see the white of your eyes
So come out of your disguise
I see the white of your eyes
And you see the tears in mine
So tell me the truth
Do you hear me?

I see the white of your eyes
This is what I advise
I see the white of your eyes
And you see the fear in mine
So tell me the truth
Do you feel me?

I see the white of your eyes
Please be more than wise
I see the white of your eyes
And you see the tears in mine
So tell me the truth
Do you love me?

Wherever You Find It

Happiness is found in the hearts of those who had a hug and handled horrible holidays by holding someone's hand. Make a habit to make it happen. Harmless harmony hates hazards, so hear a melody and don't hinder your high expectations. Don't hide the hints because someone hopes to honor your honesty. Give humor, not humiliation, to humanity. Let your happiness be your guide.

A smile is found on some faces of the shy and sometimes single. They send out strong yet simple messages that make the sun shine brighter and send the shores sailing. Silence becomes sound, and Saturday and Sunday are the days that hold the secrets. Let your smile be your umbrella.

Laughter is found in love, and sometimes even lust, leaving long-lasting goodbyes with a lullaby. Lead the way, and let the language of love be a lesson with the law of liberty. Listen, and learn not to live with lies but with life. Because life can be funny, let laughter be your medicine.

Happiness is found in a smile.
A smile is found in laughter.
Laughter is found in happiness.

Where My Secret Lies

A story untold is about to unfold

before your eyes; it's no surprise where my secret lies

My secret lies in a place that's full of grace

My secret lies in the sky where the birds and bees fly

My secret lies in the moon that goes down at noon

My secret lies in the sun; as for coldness, there is none

My secret lies in the ocean; it holds a special potion

My secret lies in the fire where heat is a desire

My secret lies in the ground where danger could be found

My secret lies in the grass where flowers grow and pass

My secret lies in the field where there is so much to build

My secret lies in the air; I think I like it there

My secret lies in the rain where there's an equal loss and gain

My secret lies in the rainbow of colors that come and go

My secret lies in the clouds because they never appear to be proud My

secret lies in the day while opportunities continue to come my way My

secret lies in the night where everything is just right

My secret lies in my voice; sometimes it has no choice

My secret lies in my hands, as precious as my hair strands

My secret lies in my feet; they are what keep the beat

My secret lies in my hips; they move as much as my lips

My secret lies in my heart. What better place to start?

My secret lies in the deepest sea; my secret lies inside of me

My secret is love and everything that it's made of

determined

not to let anger or frustration consume me

A Person in Pieces

When you look at me
Tell me, what do you see?
You think you see a whole person
But no, you don't, not actually

I am a person in pieces
Like a brand-new puzzle in a box
My life has presented happiness and smiles
But it has also presented hard knocks

A puzzle has three main pieces
But many duplicates of these three
Once they're all put together
It is then that you'll see me

The first puzzle piece of my life
That you will find in the box
Has presented happiness and smiles
But it has also presented hard knocks

The first piece is described as the edge
This piece is also my foundation
This piece is always straight
And it's the beginning of my creation

When all edges are together
All corners will connect on either side
Now you can fill in the middle
And let the foundation be your guide

The second puzzle piece of my life
That you will find in the box
Has presented happiness and smiles
But it has also presented hard knocks

The second piece has arms and legs

Sometimes one of each, sometimes two
They are used to attach to one another
And if they fit, they stick like glue

Sometimes they fit because of the color
Sometimes they fit because of the shape
Sometimes they fit for no reason at all
Either way, you don't need to use tape

The third puzzle piece of my life
That you will find in the box
Has presented happiness and smiles
But it has also presented hard knocks

The third piece has what I call pockets
A small hole inserted on the left or right
They go with the arms and legs
And they fit perfect and tight

Sometimes there's only one pocket
For the arm or leg to fit
But once you got a few of them together
You'll find that you don't want to quit

This is my life, y'all
Whether you believe me or not
I have straight edges, arms, legs, and pockets
That make up for what I got

I got years of heartache
Years of tears and pain
Sometimes I cried under the moonlight
Sometimes I danced for joy in the rain

I got bruises seen in the sunshine
And scars hidden under my skin
The hurt that lasts the longest
Is the hurt that is within

Growing up without a father

That I still don't know till this day
The molestation by Mama's new man
A price I couldn't afford to pay

Separated from my three sisters
At an age I can't even remember
So many broken relationships
With the opposite sex or opposite gender

Had to be a ward of the court
Until I turned eighteen
Had to watch Mama do drugs and get beaten
When I just wanted her to run away and get clean

This is my life, y'all
Whether you believe me or not
I have straight edges, arms, legs, and pockets
That make up for what I got

I got years of joy
Because happiness is a temporary thing
The joy of life makes me write
And the happiness makes me dance and sing

When I take a look around me
I have nothing to complain about
I can smile and smile for miles
Because I am blessed without a doubt

I got a family who loves me
Who's been there through thin and thick
I've never had to stay overnight in a hospital
Because I was never, ever that sick

I've always had clothes on my back
I've always had a roof over my head
Somebody was always feeding me
I've always had a comfortable bed
Not only did I graduate from high school

But I got my Bachelor of Arts degree
Then I went ahead and got my Master's
Because for success, this might be the key

This is my life, y'all
Whether you believe me or not
I have straight edges, arms, legs, and pockets
That make up for what I got!!!

Breaking News

We interrupt your regularly scheduled program to bring you this breaking news! Officials in the city of Going Nowhere Fast found three suspects that they are trying to rescue: an elephant in the room, a woman wearing her heart on her sleeve, and a man who won't swallow his pride. City officials tried to first rescue the elephant in the room, since the two individuals' lack of communication was the reason it was there in the first place. We interviewed the woman wearing her heart on her sleeve, and this is what she had to say:

"I feel awful and rather pissed off at myself. I put myself out there again by telling him voluntarily that I loved him. Once again, there was no feedback, no positive outcome, nothing for me to go on, to say it's gonna be this way or that way, so I'm forced to make my own judgment toward the more negative side of this situation! I cried in the midst of what I thought was lovemaking but then immediately became angry when I knew that this was it. It was just sex, and no relationship was to come out of it because he was returning to his old life in another city, in a matter of hours, leaving me here, where he left me months ago. And he was still my ex. Now I have to carry these emotions on my left sleeve and be sure not to allow him to take my emotions with him. I need my emotions for myself. It's weighing me down, this heavy heart, and he doesn't seem to care. When I said, 'I love you,' and he replied, 'Do you?' all I could do was roll over and stare into the darkness. Fool me once, shame on you; fool me twice, shame on me. I allowed him to re-open a wound that was healing. He picked at the scab he initially created, and now it's bleeding all over again. And this damn elephant won't start walking!"

She gladly let us interview her but couldn't express this to the man in question, the man who wouldn't swallow his pride. When we tried to interview him, he responded with "No comment." Witnesses tell us the man hadn't been seen since June of 2013 and then suddenly arrived at the woman's residence, out of the blue, on November 3, 2013, at approximately 8:15 p.m. His intent was to have his way with her for the next eleven hours, without speaking a word to clear up what happened in the past. According to the woman, the last thing the man told her back in

June was to find someone better than him. Now, how could she do such a thing if he pops into her life when it's convenient for him?

City officials were finally able to remove the elephant from the room and rescue the two individuals—from themselves. The public is asked to please be aware of women who are wearing their hearts on their sleeves or men who won't swallow their pride. These are very dangerous individuals and can be very harmful when approached inappropriately. They're not easily identified. They appear normal on the outside until you start to date one of these individuals and begin to peel away the layers that cover up their insecurities. Beware! Be cautious! But most importantly, the public is asked to please be genuine. Brokenhearted victims are still amongst us. We now return you to your regularly scheduled program.

Can't Poet for You

I can't poet for you today, because I'm busy being Miss:
Miss Lloyd
Miss P.R.Y.D.E.
Misunderstood
Misdiagnosed
Misrepresented
Misused
Misinformed
Misguided
Misplaced
Mistreated
"You should have been a miscarry!
Because you are a mistake!"

I told myself.

"Listen, don't follow the rules; let the rules follow you,"

I told myself.

I can't poet for you today, because I'm busy putting my makeup on in the mirror.
My makeup in the mirror is my mirror in the makeup.
Eyeshadow
Eyeliner
Blush
Foundation
Extra eyelashes
Mascara
Thicker eyebrows
Lip gloss or lipstick

I told myself, "Don't make up your face; use the face you have. It's beautiful.
Don't make up your walk; use the stride you were given. It's strong.
Don't make up your talk; use the speech you were raised with. It's deep.
Don't make up your personality; use the personality you were born with. It's genuine.
Don't make up your character; use the character you already have. It's built.
Just...be...yourself,"

I told myself.

I can't poet for you today, because I'm busy being sometimey:
Sometimes I have an overdraft.
Sometimes I'm late to work.
Sometimes I can only put $10 in my gas tank.
Sometimes I forget to take out the trash.
Sometimes I feel unworthy.
Sometimes I don't want my ends trimmed.
Sometimes I get annoyed with the drivers whose plates say Texas, New York, Iowa, Mississippi, Oregon, or Florida. Why are you here?!
Sometimes I don't wash my car for months.
Sometimes I'm up until 3 in the morning, knowing I have to get up again at 8:30.
Sometimes I really love myself.
Sometimes I talk to myself.
Sometimes I miss Saturday-morning cartoons and *Pee-wee's Playhouse*. *Reading Rainbow* and *Mister Rogers' Neighborhood* and *Sesame Street* and hell, all things PBS.
Sometimes I accidentally mix my clean clothes with my dirty clothes.
Sometimes I have a bowl of cereal for dinner.
Sometimes I daydream.
Sometimes I write poems.
Sometimes I think my pastor is talking directly to me when he's preaching.
Sometimes I pray.
Sometimes I want to go to the gym but never make it.
Sometimes I get angry with my mother.
Sometimes I just get angry, period.
Sometimes I smile.
Sometimes I smile until I laugh.
Sometimes I laugh until I cry.
Sometimes I cry like a baby.

So I can't poet for you today, maybe tomorrow...

Destruction Meant for Instruction

Initially we were building something special
Under new CONstruction
Until she came and destroyed everything
Causing great DEstruction

He decided to block any progress by creating OBstruction
Marquitta, there is a lesson to be learned from this hidden INstruction

January thirteenth, two thousand ten
The day I lost my closest friend
A day that I will never forget
He brought my fantasy world to an end

She repeatedly called my cellular phone
But she was afraid to be so grown
When I finally heard her nervous voice
It was surely a female to me unknown

She left her message on my voicemail
Whether lying or not, I couldn't tell
At this point, it didn't matter so much
Her message made me cry, scream, and yell

When I confronted him that night
I wanted to physically hurt him on sight
But it took everything inside of me
To do what I felt was right

Initially we were building something special
Under new CONstruction
Until she came and destroyed everything
Causing great DEstruction

He decided to block any progress by creating OBstruction
Marquitta, there is a lesson to be learned from this hidden INstruction

Immediately forgave him for his selfish act
Had to do it to keep self intact
Without forgiveness, they'd both have control
They would win and I would lose; this is a fact

Thinking we'd be together forever
His plan to hurt me was really quite clever
It hurt me beyond my heart and my soul
Will I ever get over this pain? Maybe never

February nineteenth, he came to a decision
Deciding his fate based on my vision
Deciding only to be my friend
Now my world was a chaotic collision

He forced his goodbyes when I was nineteen
He left me untouched and completely clean
Am I forced to let him go again?
So unheard of, as it was unseen

Initially we were building something special
Under new CONstruction
Until she came and destroyed everything
Causing great DEstruction

He decided to block any progress by creating OBstruction
Marquitta, there is a lesson to be learned from this hidden INstruction

There is no possible way for this to be fair
Turn off my feelings and pretend I don't care
I've loved this man since he first walked in my life
You want me to believe love is still in the air?

Bull, he's a liar; he doesn't love me
He tricked me into believing this is where he wanted to be
Imagine loving someone who can't love you back
From this suffering and agony, I just want to be free

What am I to do, a woman full of scorn?
He played me for a fool and now I'm broken and torn

Would I be wrong to want sweet revenge?
Damaged goods, used, forsaken, weak, and worn

We got the same gifts, both sat in the passenger's seat
Spent holidays with both of us, but how could I compete?
We were taken shopping and saw the same venues
Even took us to the same restaurant to eat

Initially we were building something special
Under new CONstruction
Until she came and destroyed everything
Causing great DEstruction

He decided to block any progress by creating OBstruction
Marquitta, there is a lesson to be learned from this hidden INstruction

What he was doing for me, he was doing for her too
He got in my pants and her pants more than a few
I guess we were two more notches in his belt
How could I not see in front of me so true?

Someone please tell me how to get past this
Something that started with just a plain kiss
He won't let go of my faded, broken heart
So much about us I'll always miss

I want to erase these memories from my mind
I wish I could press stop and then press rewind
A nightmare I'm reliving over and over again
From someone so cold-hearted and so unkind

From fantasy to reality, I finally am awake
What I thought was real turned out to be fake
I gave him all of me, all of the time
It's time I get all of me back, and TAKE!!

Initially we were building something special
Under new CONstruction
Until she came and destroyed everything

Causing great DEstruction

He decided to block any progress by creating OBstruction
Marquitta, there is a lesson to be learned from this hidden INstruction

My mind wants me to hate him so bad
My heart won't let me; I continue to feel sad
Once again, love teases, points, and laughs
Because of what I once thought I had

I still cry at night and at least once a day
When I feel tears coming, I just try to pray
I wish things were normal; I want him back
How can this happen and what do I say?

Both their messages replay in my head
When I'm moving around and while I'm in bed
I felt so alive when we were together
Now I often wonder if I'm better off dead

"I'm not going anywhere," is what he would claim
I wonder if to her he said the same
When he opened his mouth, he fed me a lie
He played me like a game; ain't it a shame?

Initially we were building something special
Under new CONstruction
Until she came and destroyed everything
Causing great DEstruction

He decided to block any progress by creating OBstruction
Marquitta, there is a lesson to be learned from this hidden INstruction

Just because you're together long
It doesn't mean the two of you will stay strong
The fork in the road divided us
And I wonder where the two of us went wrong

He would have kept cheating had I never found out
His fun was snatched away, no doubt

Unfortunately for me, I still love him so
Even though I know what he's really about

After this tragedy, can I trust another man?
He stole my heart from me and he ran
He told me we could work this out
Yet and still alone I stand

I know it's my fault; I gave him an ultimatum
And because of his decision, now I almost hate him

Initially we were building something special, under new CONstruction
Until she came and destroyed everything, causing great DEstruction

He decided to block any progress by creating OBstruction
Marquitta, there is a lesson to be learned from this hidden INstruction

Haiku

Truth was a stranger
As I rested next to lies
He never loved me

Heartbreak Hotel

She arrived at the hotel just as sure as you please
On time, I might add, with her mind at ease

She stepped out of the cab as a smile drew upon her face
She said to herself, "I remember this place."

It was only twelve months ago when she was last here
Since the place looked the same, it couldn't have been just a year

She was meeting her "Mister"; she was thought of as the "mistress"
He was married when they first met; she couldn't be any less

He had been divorced now for six months or more
He wanted to meet her again at the same place as before

She located the front desk after she entered the hotel
This place was always high class, not like any ordinary motel

She said to the lady behind the desk, "I need the key for room #8;
I'm meeting my Mister there, and I cannot be late."

She asked herself, "Why call him Mister? He's now a single man."
She preferred calling him "Mister" because she was his biggest fan

Room #8 is where they last met; the key even looked the same
She remembered where the room was, and she was glad that she came

She was very excited to see her "Mister" again
She stuck her key in the door and couldn't wait to get in

"I know he has not changed, with his mustache and dimple."
She thought to herself, "This man was never simple."

She opened up the door, and what did she find?
Her Romeo, her "Mister," was still so unkind

The carpet was clean, and the bed was neatly made
The curtains were slightly opened, and an envelope rested on the lamp shade

Before she approached the envelope, she looked for her "Mister"
She thought to herself, "He's treating me like a stepsister."
"Mister, I'm here," she said as she knocked on the bathroom door

And there was no answer, so she began to pace the floor

She looked back at the letter that was waiting to be read
She could feel her eyes begin to water, "He'd better just be late," she said.
She hesitated for a moment before she picked up the letter
"He didn't stand me up," she cried, "because I know better."

As she peeled open the envelope, a piece of paper caught her eye
"He didn't stand me up," she cried again. "This is all a lie!"

She began to unfold the letter as she wiped away her tears
She knew in this letter she'd face her greatest fears

The first words she read struck her right in the heart
"My Dearest Mistress," she read. "I'm sorry that we had to part.

This letter was written only for your benefit.
It will hurt me more than it will you; I wish I could change every bit.

My lady gave me a call, so my mistress you can no longer be.
I know you anticipated my hug; I know you wanted to see me.

We have two children together, and I still love my wife.
Everything was good with you, but I have another life.

So throw this letter away, and forget about what we had.
If you can help it, my dear, please, please don't be sad.

One of these days another mister may come along.
I just can't stay with you; that would be all wrong.

Try and understand me; understand why I'm doing this.
I'll miss your tender hugs, and I'll miss your sweet kiss.

She told me she still loved me, and then I kissed her.
So goodbye, my dear friend. Sincerely, your Mister."

Her tears wet the paper as she carried it to the trash.
"This is the last time," she said, "Heartbreak Hotel will get my damn cash."

He Couldn't Finish...

He couldn't finish breaking my heart fast enough.
Obviously, he didn't cause enough cracks and splits for his satisfaction.
But, then, to watch me pick up the broken pieces scattered amongst my soul was a bit humorous to him.
How could someone that looks like you, walks and talks like you, be such a cruel you? I asked.
With a blank stare, he said…nothing.
With blood-stained hands that trembled, I gathered the pieces and carried them under my left arm.
Until further notice, heart is closed for repairs

He Was...

Because he was the wrong person
Saying all the right things,
I presented him with my presence

While his presence was always absent
I "lied" next to the truth, and his truth
Continued to lie to me

So while I was coping with the chaos
In my conscious mind,
He said to me

"You'll never meet another man like me."
I responded with,
"I hope not…"

I Heard You Were Leaving

I heard you were leaving
It's not a surprise
You already knew
You're of the chosen guys

I heard you were leaving
To find a new life
You'll meet someone special
Whom you'll make your wife

I heard you were leaving
Don't forget about me
Because to my heart
You own a special key

I heard you were leaving
May God bless your heart
Because in my life
You're an important part

I heard you were leaving
Take care of yourself
Learn all you can
Bring back your wealth

I heard you were leaving
I won't be sad
But I will admit
You're the best guy I've ever had

I heard you were leaving
I'll be all right
Thoughts in the day
Dreams at night

I heard you were leaving
I can't come with you

I'm wishing you luck
Praying for you too

I heard you were leaving
Our memories I'll keep
My feelings for you
Grew so very deep

I heard you were leaving
Let's share one last kiss
There's nothing about you
That I will not miss

I heard you were leaving
I feel much fear
You'll be far away
Phone calls will keep you near

I heard you were leaving
No more left to say
I thank God we were able
To spend together one last day

I heard you were leaving
I'll smile; I won't cry
Because we both know
How hard it is to say goodbye

Massacre

While bullet holes pierced the church walls,
The community sat in mourning in the halls

Emanuel African Methodist Episcopal Church existed since 1816
Nine victims took their last breath here, and the shooter escaped the scene

Cynthia Hurd, 54
Susie Jackson, 87
Ethel Lance, 70
Rev. DePayne Middleton, 49
Hon. Rev. Clementa Pinckney, 41
Tywanza Sanders, 26
Rev. Daniel Simmons, Sr., 74
Rev. Sharonda Singleton, 45
Myra Thompson, 59

Murdered by the hands of Dylan Storm Roof, 21
Wednesday evening in June of 2015 in Charleston

Is it a coincidence that each victim had a black face,
While the shooter had a white face? It's not my place

To judge, to ponder, to cry
To wonder and to ask why

Do you think God gave them a sign while they studied their Bibles?
There was no way they even anticipated Roof's sudden arrival

On Roof's 21st birthday he purchased a .45 caliber gun
He wasn't cleared for the purchase, but the crime cannot be undone

Inspired by the Council of Conservative Citizens, white supremacy
He stepped foot into their Bible study, disrupting their intimacy

Researching conservative citizens, Roof concluded Negroes have lower IQs

After a 14-hour manhunt, it was time he paid society its dues

Roof sat with them for 60 minutes before the slaughter
Taking the life of a father, son, brother, mother, sister, and daughter

Roof left one survivor because he needed someone to tell the story
I pray those nine victims' souls made it to glory

Thank God for Debbie Dills, who spotted him while driving in her car
She followed him for 35 miles, not knowing if he'd continue to go far

Roof was on suicide watch after being placed in a bulletproof vest
Officers knew it wasn't enough for him to just be under arrest

Family members recognized that Roof tore their family apart
They still chose to forgive him from the bottom of their heart

His friend, Joey Meek, was charged with concealing evidence
Roof told Meek about a six-month plan of race war; now it makes sense

Judge James B. Gosnell held the first official court hearing by video
Roof was only able to participate by way of audio

The judge set Roof's bond at one million dollars, no more, no less
Now do you think Roof's life is over? What a complete mess!

My Heart

When your heart speaks louder than your head
Do you listen to every word that is said?
Or do you ignore one or the other instead?

When your heart speaks louder than your head
Do you holler and scream out loud?
Or do you quietly hide in the crowd?

When your heart speaks louder than your head
Do you cry out to be rescued?
Or do you curse and be nasty and rude?

When your heart speaks louder than your head
Do you punish the person by your side?
Or do you let your tears be your guide?

When your heart speaks louder than your head
Do you do what is thoughtful and clever?
Or do you react, always or never?

When your heart speaks louder than your head
Do you relieve stress through rhyme?
Or do you let yourself run out of time?

When your heart speaks louder than your head
Do you shut it up with a gun?
Or do you walk away until you begin to run and run and run and run
and run....?

My Life Lesson

Experience was the teacher; I was the student.
My classroom didn't have four walls, no desks, no whiteboards, and no overhead projectors.

I filled my backpack with old memories of heartbreaks, anger, disappointments, and frustrations in a place and time when alcohol and a booty call didn't mix.

I filled my backpack with tears you put in my eyes because of all your lies.
But the truth is I allowed you to because I loved you, boo!

My notebook had very few blank pages in it because I made sure every college-ruled paper had my mistake written on it, so I could physically see it, mentally memorize it, and never do it again.

Unfortunately, I couldn't use my pencil to rewrite my curse that I didn't rehearse.
I couldn't erase the mistake I made in life, like I can erase my words on paper and start over again,
or maybe rewrite it with a pen.

But if I make a mistake with my pen, will the Wite-Out really make the mistake go away?
Nope! That mistake is here to stay.

Sure, I can cover it up and write over it,
But just like the scars I so proudly earned, I learned; oh, yeah, I learned.

I couldn't hold it together, like I held six or seven pages together with a paper clip or a staple.
And if I missed a page, I'd have to use my staple remover to remove the thin metal holding everything together.

Now I would have permanent holes that resemble the holes to the left of my notebook paper, only smaller.

And when I re-staple, I won't be capable of putting the staple in the same place twice.
Although that would be nice.
Can I make the same mistake twice?

Possibly. But just like no two days are the same,
no two mistakes will know my name.
But I am to blame
for I did the research; I studied you; I learned you.
Sometimes I even copied you and reprinted you.

I engraved you in my mind and Photoshopped you in my heart.
I took notes on my index cards, highlighting the important memories from my history book.

My notes are made up of words that are four and five letters long,
when some of them should have been eight.
And I hate when I forget to put the date.

I have to remember when I was exposed to this lesson.
The important memories are what keep me focused,
but that's all they are, memories....

My history book was a textbook of memories to remind me of where I've been and why I left.
How I got there will always be a mystery,
but where I'm going, we'll just have to wait and see.

A history book was the only textbook I carried.
I didn't need an English book because I already knew the language.
I didn't need a science book because I already knew the facts.
I didn't need a mathematics book because I already knew how to count.
After all, just one textbook was the right amount, right?

Wrong, because I knew all along that the song that was forced out from between my lips and danced off my tongue was only a playback of the heartbreaks, anger, disappointments, and frustrations that eventually led to depression because I was tired of learning.

So, yes, I did need yet another textbook to read from cover to cover and

teach me a lesson!
My brain, by now, had gained enough wrinkles to enforce pain and
increase my desire to stay sane.
These main lessons were training lessons; they weren't in-vain lessons
but how-to-make-it-through-the-rain lessons.

But my rain wasn't a few drops from a grey sky;
it was a storm with thunder, lightning, and small chunks of ice that one
might call hail.
And I lived in H-E-L-L, breathed it, in-helled, it and ex-helled it.

Hell, it wasn't a letter someone sent to me in the mail;
it was more like a tale someone told me once about experience.
And now I know it oh too well.

My history book is the only textbook I used,
not knowing that it would keep me amused
and entertained with fulfilling knowledge.

Now I'm being truthfully accused of learning too damn much.
I didn't abuse or misuse my education.
I learned my lesson and turned my lesson into an earned lesson.
A life lesson.

Passing the Graveyard

I passed by the graveyard today
Thank God I wasn't dropped off
I've lied and I've managed to deceive
The things I've done, you wouldn't believe

My thoughts are evil
And I curse those who love me
Then I cry all night
Because I feel so unhappy

My thoughts are dangerous
I pray I don't do the things I think
I'm warning them to be careful
I may hurt them in a blink

My heart has so much hatred
I resent what they say and do
They keep hurting me deep inside
So I have the right to hurt them, too

My heart is definitely not right
They're making my life a challenge
They're pushing me away from them
And this is going to be my revenge

My mouth can be uncontrollable
I say things that I shouldn't
Sometimes I mean it and sometimes I don't
Things come out of my mouth that normally wouldn't

My mouth can be like a weapon
I may say things they don't want to hear
But if what I'm saying is the truth
I want it to be loud and clear

I passed by the graveyard today
Maybe I should have been dropped off

I've lied and I've managed to deceive
The things I've done, you wouldn't believe

Thank You for Changing My Life

Thank you for changing my life
It may never be the same again
You were once such a close friend
Fortunately, I still want you around even until the very end

Thank you for changing my life
You said you had my best interest
I wonder if it was just a test
I guess I failed to study because unfortunately I didn't do my best

Thank you for changing my life
I thought we went together well
What better match than male and female
But nothing's ever perfect; this must be the true meaning of hell

Thank you for changing my life
I thought you had my back
Instead, you settled in for an attack
Even though you knew I was vulnerable, no matter what I seemed to lack

Thank you for changing my life
Although I knew somehow you would
You did more than I thought you should
I must say you surprised me instead; you tricked me as only you could

Thank you for changing my life
I used to carry you in my heart
You and I were never apart
Now that we are separated, it forces me to make a new start

Thank you for changing my life
I remember when I trusted you
But it was too good to be true
Why should I question your motive? You did what you were supposed to do
Thank you for changing my life

You really took me for a ride
I went up, down, side to side
It was such a wonderful adventure; I didn't want to run and hide

Thank you for changing my life
I don't talk like I used to talk
I can't walk like I used to walk
You really gave me a makeover; I'm outlined with special chalk

Thank you for changing my life
You absolutely made me fall
But I had to answer your call
It was fun while it lasted; no need to complain at all

Thank you for changing my life
Now my edges have been made rough
My skin is thicker and tough
It's all over for me now; I can't take it anymore; I've had enough

Thank you for changing my life
No more tears; no more crying
I give up; I'm done trying
Keep whatever it is you got; whatever you're selling, I ain't buying

Thank you for changing my life
I've experienced a new change
But it's all right; I don't find it strange
Now I know what I have to do; there are some priorities I must rearrange

Thank you for changing my life
I'm gonna hold my head up high
I know I'd rather live than die
It's hard to hear the truth sometimes, but I don't want to hear another lie

Thank you for changing my life
You've forced me to run this race

Even though there are challenges to face

I just want to complete the task; I don't have to make first place

Thank you for changing my life
You used to be real good to me
And I was the best that I could be
But none of this really matters if you're blind and just can't see

Thank you for changing my life
Now I have the strength to be strong
How could something so right be so wrong?
I don't even know how to be free because you held me captive for so long

Thank you for changing my life
You taught me that I can handle anything
It doesn't matter what life may bring
After all, nothing's too hard for God; I'd rather shout than sing

You may be asking yourself, "What change is she speaking of?"
How do you reach below for what's up above?
If you haven't figured it out, what I'm talking about is "love"

So thank you, "love," for changing my life
I'm much better than I was before
I know I must be a soldier to the core
Because I survived what you put me through
Thanks to you, I don't believe in love anymore!!

That Chick

I was never supposed to meet her
For she was the cause of my humiliation
He was cheating on me with her
So began the process of elimination

You might think I was over it by now
After all, it only happened in 2010
But when it's out of sight, it's out of mind
And the God in me is still trying to be his friend

With the intent to conduct business with him
Perhaps that was also a mistake
But I promise you, I had no other intentions
And I never wanted to appear fake

Lord knows I had no idea
Of what was actually about to take place
The one who was the other woman
And I were about to come face to face

When it all went down back then
I needed to maintain my composure
Even though the pieces of my heart
Were now in a state of exposure

I heard about that chick
That went crazy over some dude
And I never wanted to be that chick
Because I always thought that chick was rude

That chick cursed out the girl
And she cursed him out, too
So I didn't wanna be that chick
He wasted her time; this she knew

That chick slashed his tires

And she slashed all four
So I didn't wanna be that chick
I called her stupid to the core

That chick busted his windshield
She may have used a brick or a bat
So I didn't wanna be that chick
I called her a spoiled brat

That chick keyed his driver's side
So he would always remember with confidence
So I didn't wanna be that chick
I called her ridiculous and said she had no sense

That chick stalked him indeed
Went places she knew he'd be
So I didn't wanna be that chick
I always said that wouldn't be me

That chick talked to her homeboys
Set him up to get him jumped
So I didn't wanna be that chick
I said she deserved to be dumped

That chick went on Facebook and Twitter
And told on him like a true snitch
So I didn't wanna be that chick
I called her a b*tch

So I was never supposed to meet her
For she was the cause of my humiliation
This that chick that he cheated on me with
So began the process of elimination

As I stated, I was trying to conduct business
Only to find out this chick is now his roommate
Now I'm trying to keep myself
From turning into that chick I love to hate

Now I wanna be that chick

That chick I talked so badly about
I wanna do all the hurtful things that chick did to him
And piss him off, no doubt

But the God in me won't let me
Simply because it happened in 2010
And I forgave him already
So that I could just be his friend

There's a chick I didn't mention
She prays for his story
That's the chick that I am
Because I wanna meet Jesus in glory

This Is Some Bullsh**!

I just paid my car note
Paid my insurance and my rent
Gave my tithes and offering to the church
Now my pockets got a new dent
You telling me I can't buy a new outfit?
Forgive me, Lord, but this is some bullsh**!

My boss stay on my back
She won't give me a break
Did I mention?
They paying me little to nothing
I can't even afford to pay attention
Don't wanna stay, but can't afford to quit
Forgive me, Lord, but this is some bullsh**!

My dude and I ain't getting along
He just don't wanna act right
I hate it when we argue
I hate it when we fight
And I'm supposed to believe our relationship is legit?
Forgive me, Lord, but this is some bullsh**!

My sister don't come around
Because she owes me money
And when I ask her about it
She get to being funny
I gave her a loan to get her out of a pit
Forgive me, Lord, but this is some bullsh**!

Friends start acting like enemies
When you can't afford to pay their bills
Look, that ain't my responsibility
And you ain't stressin' me out, 'cause stress kills
Sometimes what you ask for is exactly what you get
Forgive me, Lord, but this is some bullsh**!
My school done raised tuition

Now I gotta pay for my own books
I gotta pay for all my classes too?
I wish I could go to school on my own good looks
All I'm trying to do is learn a little bit
Forgive me, Lord, but this is some bullsh**!

My car done broke down again
Now public transportation gotta be my ride
And you can't use your transfer more than once
Because it don't work; believe me — I tried
Got places to go, so let me find a place to sit
Forgive me, Lord, but this is some bull sh**!

Damn it, I forgot to pay my phone bill
Now my cell done got cut off
Wish my sneeze could reconnect it
Or maybe even my darn cough
I gotta have my phone; I can't live without it
Forgive me, Lord, but this is some bullsh**!

Can't eat no more fried chicken
Because my cholesterol is high
Got thyroid disease, and diabetes runs in my family
So I keep exercising just to get by
I take medication like I'm gettin' a hit
Forgive me, Lord, but this is some bullsh**!

Won't celebrate Father's Day
Because, hell, I don't even know the cat
He don't deserve to be called a man
Because he was never that
I wish kids could come with a two-parent kit
Forgive me, Lord, but this is some bullsh**!

I catch hell like you catch a cold
I catch stress like a blister is bold
The devil be holding me hostage like a catcher holds his mitt
Forgive me, Lord, but this is some bullsh!**

When the Pain Is All Over You

Sink full of dishes
Mind full of wishes
What's a girl to do
When the pain is all over you?

Don't give me no Bayer
It'll just make me act sly
Don't give me no Benadryl
It'll just make me shy

Don't give me no Tylenol
It'll just make me wanna fly
Don't give me no Advil
It'll just make me high

Don't give me no NyQuil
It'll just make me cry
Don't give me no DayQuil
It'll just make me dry

Don't give me no Excedrin
It'll just make me lie
Don't give me no penicillin
It'll just make me you, not I

Don't give me no Theraflu
It'll just make me ask why
Don't give me no aspirin
It'll just make me pry

Don't give me no Milk of Magnesia
It'll just make me want your guy
Don't give me no Pepto Bismol
It'll just make me hit you in your eye

Don't give me no Dexeryl
It'll just make me pass you by

Don't give me no laxative
It'll just make me say "My, oh my."

Don't give me no Midol
It'll just make me sigh
Don't give me no Aleve
It'll just make me wanna die

Hell, don't give me no medication
It won't do me no good
It won't do anything for me
That the label says it should

So I think I'll just sit here instead
Thinking I might be better off dead
With a sink full of dishes
And a mind full of wishes

So what's a girl to do
When the pain is all over you?

encouraged
by prayer, the church, and God

Conversations with the Devil

You know who I am. You know who I am. I knew you'd be back. You couldn't stay away too long. You know what I aim to do; it ain't no secret. I aim to kill, steal, and destroy, and not necessarily in that order. So, ultimately, when I'm done with you, I will have killed you, stolen from you, and destroyed you from the inside out. You know me. I'm not that fictional character with a red pitchfork, pointy ears, and a long red tail. I look just like your neighbor. I look like your co-worker. I look like your friend. I even look like your family member. You know me. And I know you. I know your weakness. And I know you're phony. So don't come at me with those childish games, acting like this is the "last time." That's what you said the last time. You know me. I got everything you want and everything you don't need. Just say the word: sex, envy, greed, unhappiness! Whatever you don't need, I got it! I can present it to you on a silver platter. And you'll be so pleased when it's all over that you'll be begging me for more. Never mind that voice in your head that you call your conscience. It ain't got nothing to do with what we got going on here. Never mind that nudge in your heart that you call the holy spirit. It ain't got nothing to do with what we got going on here. I got you. You know I got you. You might think you wanna escape, but naw, I got you wrapped around me so tight that I can't even breathe. Hahahahaha, I love to see you coming with your sad eyes and your thirsty lips. That's what I'm here for. To hurt you, I mean to help you. To help you hurt yourself, that is. I don't need to hear the reasons that brought you back here again. I don't care! Just come on over here so I can show you what I can do. That backbone you think you got, naw, that ain't stoppin' me. You thought you had strength to defeat me, but oh no, you lost this fight before it even got started. Speaking of starting, let me start you off with a little lust for your appetizer, followed by some hate, envy, and backbiting for dinner. And awwww, look what I have for dessert—revenge!

Don't apologize; it's okay to want these things. It's okay to act this way. I got you. Oh, and when you're done, send some of your friends my way. I'd love to entertain some fresh, naive minds like yours. How enticing! But when you consider which friends you're bringing, you be sure to leave that Jesus guy at the house. I've tried to play with Him before and

He ain't no fun. But do bring me your closest lady friends, your homeboys, your sisters and brothers, aunts and uncles — heck, bring me your mama and her mama too! But leave that Jesus guy at the house. He don't play fair. I don't need that type of energy around here. But you — I'll take you and everything you think you are. Because I do know you're nothing without Him, but you're everything without me so...I guess that means I need you, huh? Yep, you caught me. I do need you. I need you to help me destroy the kingdom and tear down the house of G---G---G---G---God — I can't even say it. Help me to tear down that house, because this is where it's at. This is what's up. You can't deny it; you love it! You love me, don't you? Yeah, I heard you confessing to your "God" the other day, saying how much you loved Him, but as soon as you had a disaster, as soon as someone let you down, here you come, running my direction, and I welcomed you with open arms, just like I always do. So why should this time be any different? I know when you're coming, so I just wait for you. And you never cease to amaze me. When I'm done with you, when you're all used up and beat up and broken and torn down from our adventures, I'll let you go because I know you'll be back. Oh, you ain't coming back this time? Hmmm, we'll see. Run on! Yeah, that Jesus man is carrying you now, but just wait...if you don't come back, I got your sister and your mama over here, and they'll do whatever I say because they ain't never hung out with that Jesus dude, anyway. So you go on. No, don't try to come back and get them. They are mine. Didn't you hear? I came to steal and — you know the rest. And I just stole your folks. Boo hoo, what you gonna do? Tell your God on me? Tell Him and see if He can snatch these phonies away from me. I dare Him. I dare you! (To be continued......)

I Don't Fit In

I don't fit in, so I stick out

You really don't know who I am or what I'm all about
Shaking my head at you and laughing out loud
Because you appear foolish and I'm peacock proud

I don't fit in, so I stick out

You inhale those cancer sticks
and they make me sick
so I look for air quick;
I watch you put it to your lips,
then flick; how I wish that habit you'd kick
sorry, I don't smoke cigarettes

I don't fit in, so I stick out

You sip from a bottle or can, the most colorful drink
And then your personality changes, I think;
as you rush to the sink,
I sigh and I wink.
Sorry, I don't consume alcohol; watch and don't blink

I don't fit in, so I stick out

Sometimes, like a sailor, you curse;
your words of choice are the worst
when there is so much more to language in our universe;
before you practice, let's rehearse
you carrying your purse
like a lady, and watching what you say, okay?
I'm sorry, I swear I am! I just don't talk that way.

I don't fit in, so I stick out

When I'm asleep, I usually sleep alone,
not with a man to me unknown;
yeah, I'm grown,
grown enough to make adult decisions, but if it's wrong,
it's wrong. I ain't saying I never got caught up, but I didn't stay caught up for long.
I most definitely get weak, but my strength comes once I'm strong —
Strong enough to sleep with me, myself, and I. Don't cry.
Just because I'm alone don't mean I'm lonely.
Sorry, I sleep alone, not around, so don't mistake me for being phony.

I don't fit in, so I stick out

I like to go out and enjoy myself, but my clubb'n' days are done
still have fun
with several or just one.
Or just me until the sun
rises or sets and I've run
out of ideas, so I guess you won.
Sorry, I don't club like that no more, son!

I don't fit in, so I stick out

To me, you stress
to hike up my dress
so I can impress
and wear my heels six inches high
instead of three inches, why?
I can pick up a man in my pajamas and on my worst hair day.
What can I say?
I'm beautiful anyway
and be that as it may,
I can catch a "boyfriend" today
but a husband is for whom I pray.
There's a difference, if you look at it that way.

I don't fit in, so I stick out

My attire
is not for hire.
The woman in me is who you should admire
so you won't make me into a liar.
I don't need to dress like you to get attention.
But that tells me your smile or personality is not enough to mention
and there's too much tension.
I'm good just the way I am.
I'm sorry if my clothing makes you uncomfortable, ma'am.
We all got sorrow and pains;
we all think with our brains
and we all got blood pumping through our veins.
I'd get along with everyone when it comes to being myself
If everyone stayed in their own lanes.

I don't fit in, so I stick out

Just Call on Jesus

When skies are blue but you are too
Just call on Jesus; He'll see you through

When times are bad and they make you sad
Just call on Jesus; He'll make you glad

When things get rough and then get tough
Just call on Jesus; He knows when burdens are enough

When situations get in your way and you're looking for a brighter day
Just call on Jesus; He'll hear you when you pray

When problems get you down and there's no friend around
Just call on Jesus; He is easily found

When you have a broken heart and your world is torn apart
Just call on Jesus; He'll give you a new start

When happiness ends and anger begins
Remember that Christ paid the cost

He bled and died for our sins
When He hung on the rugged cross

Life Support

My heart is where my emotions lie...
Or where they tell the truth, if you will
God's got me on life support
Because it was me you tried to kill
But God is keeping me alive, still

God's got me on life support
Because I'm hanging on by a thread
Holding on to what's left of my life
And what's right of my life instead
Because at this point, I'm almost dead

He's holding on to both my hands
And He's holding on to me tight
He's pulling me out of the darkness
And into the marvelous light
Opening my eyes when I was without sight

I'm crying out for some strength
Because I believe He hears me when I pray
If I continue to hide in the midnight hour
Then I'll never see the light of day
So He gotta hear everything I say

God's got me on life support
So I suppose this is part of His plan
I assume that's why I should love Him
And trust no breathing man
God keeps me like no one else can

Sometimes peace is so hard to find
Like with me it's playing hide and seek
I search in the most common places
Until what I find is myself getting weak
In this building there's a leak

Now my soul has got to move
Is there somewhere a better location
Where I can lay my burdens down?
I'm sure He included it in His creation
Allowing me the perfect destination

God's got me on life support
And He's supporting my life like it's something great
Let Him put you on life support
Take this time with me to participate
Don't let your fate be said too late

We can never go under our problems
But we have to go through them
Before we can get over them

Love Lost

If ever I were an angel
Right here on this earth before
Only God knows where I wandered
Only God knew how I could soar

But from amongst them I came
When He called out my name
And I had to be so unusual
I was never meant to be the same

But, oh, one day as different was I
I met one who was different as me
He soared so high above the ground
That it was almost hard for me to see

But he soared, and he soared some more
To my eyes once did he appear
That as I looked up and I saw him
It was then that he was coming near

I said a word or two
To get his attention that fine day
But he smiled and he soared
Never to even look my way

Then before I could blink my eye
I heard him mumble something so sweet
"I'll come back for you; I promise
And that's when the two of us shall meet."

Oh, how excited I was, oh yes
To meet this angel of mine
He may not have belonged to me
But it still suited me just fine

I waited so impatiently now
For my angel to get back quick
And just as I was about to grin
I suddenly became crippled and sick

What is this thing happening?
I can't explain it at all

It's as if blue skies have gone away
And I'm surrounded by dirt and wall

It's suddenly really dark and gloomy
Almost-darkness is covering my view
I can't see anything or anybody
Oh, God, what must I do?

I'm crying and I'm hurt
Not knowing how to handle the pain
Now, not only is it dark and gloomy
But, oh, it's starting to rain

I begin to see flashes of lightning
On the left side of me and on the right
Then suddenly I see two creatures
Who are putting up a great fight

One of the creatures is quite ugly
And he's scary, too, might I add
But the more he shows his face to me
The more I become so sad

The other creature is something beautiful
I can't describe it, but I'll try
He's showing his face, and I feel warm
And I'm feeling aroused, without knowing why

But as the fight continues on
I'm cheering on the most beautiful man
Because I think that's the angel I saw before
When this journey of mine first began

A strike against the one so unattractive
Then a strike against the other
I was getting weaker and sicker
I wanted to call out for my mother

But it was obvious I was alone here
And I was about to be the one and only
I didn't know who was going to win this fight
But somehow I knew I was about to be lonely

And right before I could think the thought
The strongest strike came across his body so tough
I felt like I was in the struggle

Holding my heart, I yelled out, "Enough!"

But by the time I said that
It was already too late
It seemed as if it was a set-up
The devil accomplished what was fate
And I was made out to be the bait
Like Eve was in the Bible
I took a bite; yeah, I ate
And I think it cost me my mate

How could my mind be in this state?
This state of mine couldn't wait
For I had to love him on this date
He and I would walk together through a heavenly gate

But the devil killed the one I loved
And the one left standing is the one I now hate!

My Brother...My Sister

Stretch out your arms, my brother
And reach for some help
For I know you cannot do it alone

Stretch out your arms, my sister
And reach for some love
For someone cherished you as you cherish your own

Stretch out your arms, my brother
And reach for some peace
For all around you there is war

Stretch out your arms, my sister
And reach for some happiness
For if you don't, you are already destroyed to the core

Stretch out your arms, my brother
And reach for some faith
For I know you need it every day

Stretch out your arms, my sister
And reach for some strength
For I know you'll need it as you go on your way

Stretch out your arms, my brother
And reach for some courage
For this alone will defeat your every fear

Stretch out your arms, my sister
And reach for some pride
For now you can lend your voice and your ear

Stretch out your arms, my brother
And reach for some life
For this was a gift from God many centuries ago

Stretch out your arms, my sister
And reach for everything you can

For when you're done, you'll know all you need to know

My Prayer

Tonight I bow down before You
Because You blessed me today; thank You

At one in the afternoon, I prayed and went on my way
Because I didn't know what was in store for this day

I gave a homeless man five nickels at two
I later found a five dollar bill; I guess to me it was due

I said a kind word to a stranger at three
She smiled and returned a kind word to me

While crossing the street, I helped a blind man at four
Just as my enemy had to help us both get in the door

Just as the clouds grew gray, it began to sprinkle at five
And a friend offered me a ride because she knew I couldn't drive

Before getting home, I stopped for sweets at about six
And someone told me the store was just in a robbery fix

I made it home a little before seven
To find everything still in its place; my junky heaven

As I got comfortable, I began to open my mail at eight
One letter informed me my new employment begins tomorrow; I can't be late

I changed my clothes and crawled into bed at nine
Then received a call; the person I knew in the hospital would be just fine

After an hour, I turned off the television and meditated at ten
And then I read a few scriptures in case tomorrow I could not start over again

Tonight I bow down before You
Because You blessed me today; thank You

No One Is Bigger Than God

You can own diamonds that are worth a grand
And wear each of them on your hand

You can have a wardrobe that will last you a decade
And it still has not begun to fade

Still, no one, but no one, is bigger than God

You can live in a house big enough to hold ninety-nine
You can own every shoe that fits your foot just fine

You can have more money than an actual bank
At your job you are the highest to rank

Still, no one, but no one, is bigger than God

You can have eyesight that may never go bad
You may have hearing better than anyone's ever had

You can have two arms that are very strong
And with your legs in shape, you can't go wrong

Still, no one, but no one, is bigger than God

You may be in the best health you've ever been in
And you claim you're so healthy, you'll never be sick again

You can be able to drive a different vehicle every day You
can think that you're perfect in every way

Still, no one, but no one, is bigger than God

Not mom, not dad, not husband, not wife
Not even son or daughter, at least not in this life

Not even sister or brother, uncle or aunt
Down here it's not about what we want

No, not nephew or niece

Even they don't possess God's great peace

Not grandmother or grandfather, not cousin or friend
Not doctors or lawyers, preachers or teachers, and even then

There are no pets, no animals of any kind
No matter how hard you try, you won't find

Anyone, because no one, but no one, is bigger than God

Now I Pray to Love

I used to love to pray
Now I pray to love
Yes, I pray to love
Can somebody, anybody, up above
Show up and show me what you're made of?

I pray to love my enemies
Everyone has a minimum of two
This is absolutely true
If my enemy happens to be you
Then I'm praying for you, too

I pray to love my friends
I want my associates to be my friends as well
Because there is a difference. Can't you tell?
I have friends, both guys and female
"Friends, how many of us have them?" Does this ring a bell?

I pray to love my family
My grandma, aunts, and my mother
My sisters, I have no one to call my brother
My uncles and cousins are like no other
And my estranged father, if I have to name another

I pray to love my co-workers
Without my job, I couldn't pay a bill
To be employed these days is a very big deal
I hate my job though; I gotta keep it real
My supervisor has no idea how she makes me feel

I pray to love the people in my church
They keep me on the narrow and straight
They're not the ones I want to hate
Sometimes church is a must and I can't be late
With their help, I can walk through that heavenly gate

I pray to love my life
It brings me up and it brings me down
It makes me smile and it makes me frown
Life's like a roller coaster taking me around and around
I won't let the problems of life keep me bound

I used to love to pray
Now I pray to love

Our Gift

God is not our gift. He's our present, but not the present you unwrap, but the present that means right now. God loves you right now! He hung on the cross back then for all our hang-ups today. He walked the earth back then so we can run and not faint today. He died back then so we can live today. God is not our gift. He's our present, but not the present you unwrap, but the present that means right now. God loves you right now!

Peace

I decided to look for peace on this fair and glorious day
But I didn't know whom I'd talk to, or what I would say

I went to the sun and said, "Shining sun, I'm looking for peace. Where is he?"
The sun responded, "Peace, it doesn't dwell with me."

I went to the moon and said, "I need to find peace, fellow moon."
The moon responded, "Go that way; it will come to you soon."

I went to the stars and said, "Stars up above, is peace among you?"
The stars responded, "What is peace? I have no clue."

I went to the sky and said, "Blue sky, peace is so hard to find."
The sky responded, "I'm sorry; towards peace I am blind."

I went to the birds and said, "Blue birds, does peace fly with wings?"
The birds responded, "What flies? Only a few things."

I went to the trees and said, "Hello, large trees, is peace just as tall?"
The trees responded, "I know not peace at all."

I went to the grass and said, "Little grass, is peace ever so green?"
The grass responded, "What on Earth do you mean?"

I went to the flowers and said, "Roses and violets, what does peace smell like?"
The flowers responded, "We can't help you; we are on strike."

I went to the water and said, "Water in the lake, does peace have a taste?"
The water responded, "Why bring your time here to waste?"

I went to the wind and said, "Mighty wind, have you heard peace blow?"
The wind responded, "Peace is hidden somewhere I didn't go."

Then a voice from nowhere said, "Child, why do you ask?
I have created them; they have their own task."

Then I looked up at the heavens and said, "Dear Lord, can my luck be any worse?"
The Lord responded to me quickly, "My child, you should have come to me first."

The Sermon

The first thing I noticed was your off-green jacket
It held about seven or eight buttons in a row
Covering a checkered blue-and-white collared shirt without a tie
Were you aware that you weren't matching? Did you know?

Your checkered shirt was neatly tucked into your tan pants And
your tan pants were held up by your belt, black
Your voice was low; then your voice was high
So upon my face a smile began to crack

Maybe your jewelry was supposed to match your belt
Because on your left wrist, your watch was black, too
With the microphone in your right hand
You're preaching and telling us what we should do

When you finally stepped down from the pulpit
I noticed your pointy shoes that were brown
You weren't tall, maybe standing about 5'6"
But I saw your shoes because I happened to look down

Out of excitement, you decided to remove your jacket
That's when I noticed the ring of sweat
Unfortunately your left armpit, your right armpit
And the back of your checkered shirt were wet

Shaking my head in embarrassment
Thinking you had to feel sticky and hot
Wishing you could relax and cool off a bit
I wanted to run up and fan you a lot

Noticing your dark face looking at us
Coupled with your dark-colored hair
Confessing you preached a good word, minister
But I'll admit that my role was quite unfair

I enjoyed your sermon, but I must declare
I only heard every other word; it's true
Because my eyes were focused on what you were wearing

Instead of opening my ears to listen to you

The Visitors

One day I had way too many visitors

Fear
Shame
Doubt
Depression
and Confusion
all came knocking on my door

Fear sat on my couch
Shame slept in my bed
Doubt ate at my kitchen table
Depression bathed in my bathtub
And confusion watched my television

I didn't know what to do
My place was so crowded
I wanted them to leave
So one by one I politely asked:

"Fear, can you please get off of my couch?"
He did nothing but increase his slouch

"Shame, can you please get out of my bed?"
He then requested a thicker pillow for his head

"Doubt, can you please get up from my kitchen table?"
He continued to eat and eat as much as he was able

"Depression, can you please get out of my bathtub?"
He said, "I like it here, rub-a-dub-dub."

"Confusion, can you please turn off my television?"
He asked, "What channel do I watch?"
He needed to make a decision

They all ignored my cry
They all ignored my plea
Until I looked in the mirror
And saw that they were all a part of me

"Dear God!" I cried out,

"Please make me new."
Then, with a knock on my heart
God said, "Open up and I will help you."

I cried out again,
"Lord, please come in, quick.
These people in me
are making me sick."

God said, "My child, vengeance is mine;
I will remove them at once, and you will be just fine."

Before I could blink
I saw God move
And when he was all done
He had nothing left to prove

He grabbed Fear by the ear
And Shame by the hair
He looked at Doubt
And Doubt disappeared into thin air
He kicked Depression out the door
So Confusion became very afraid
So he passed out on the floor and died where he laid

I was so thankful to God
For all He had done
The devil was defeated
And victory had won

As He wiped away my tear
He handed me a Bible
He said to me softly,
"Should they try to return,
Use my word against them;
It is very reliable."

Made in the USA
Middletown, DE
01 March 2023